ISRAEL
TRIUMPH OF THE SPIRIT

ISRAEL
TRIUMPH OF THE SPIRIT

Delilah Shapiro

MetroBooks

MetroBooks

An Imprint of Friedman/Fairfax Publishers

© 1997 by Michael Friedman Publishing Group, Inc.

Library of Congress Cataloging-in-Publication Data available upon request.
ISBN 1-56799-446-6

Editors: Nathaniel Marunas and Celeste Sollod
Art Director: Jeff Batzli
Design: Jeff Batzli and Charles Donahue
Photography Editor: Karen L. Barr
Production Manager: Jeanne Hutter
Color separations by HK Scanner Arts Int'l Ltd.
Printed in China by Leefung-Asco Printers Ltd.

10 9 8 7 6 5 4 3 2 1

For bulk purchases and special sales, please contact:
Friedman/Fairfax Publishers
Attention: Sales Department
15 West 26th Street
New York, NY 10010
212/685-6610 FAX 212/685-1307

Visit our website:
http://www.metrobooks.com

For my parents, Harris and Frayda

Contents

Part One

The History

Introduction: *The Land of Milk and Honey*

The nation of Israel is fifty years old, but the story of how it came into existence encompasses nearly 6,000 years of Jewish history.

The land of Israel is as ancient as the sand that blows across the faded mosaic tiles at Masada, as old as the wind that rustles the lush gardens of Haifa, as powerful as the walls that surround the old city of Jerusalem, and as profound as the basic tenets of Judaism upon which the nation was founded. The story of Israel is a story of prosperity in the desert—a literal desert as well as a wasteland of wandering, assimilation, and loss. It is a tale of a nation's will to exist against all odds, a will to survive in the face of adversity. It is a story of religious faith and cultural evolution, of the sheer force of spirit that has made modern Israel into a thriving, powerful, bountiful nation, a land of milk and honey: the promised land.

The Wailing Wall, as it is now known, has become the most important Jewish religious shrine in the Old City of Jerusalem. When the second Temple was destroyed by the conquering Romans in 70 C.E., this retaining wall of the Temple Mount (at the site of which tradition says Abraham almost sacrificed his son Isaac) was all that remained of the holy structure. Devout worshipers pray at the stones of the wall, and many visitors to this holy place press slips of paper inscribed with prayers into the crevices between the rocks.

From roughly 70 C.E., when the second great Temple of Jerusalem was destroyed by Roman invaders and the Jewish people were conquered, until 1948, when the State of Israel was reestablished in the lands of the Middle East then known as Palestine, the Jews were wanderers, nomadic exiles in a largely hostile world. When the Temple of Jerusalem (of which the Western or Wailing Wall is the sole remaining part) was torn down, it is said, a shard of its stone broke away and entered the heart of every Jew, and for almost 2,000 years that stone in their hearts was their only country. Dispersed throughout Europe and the Middle East (and in later centuries the Americas), buffeted by politics and hatred wherever they attempted to settle, the story of the Jews has always been one of triumph in the face of adversity.

The early history of the Jews is preserved in the pages of the Old Testament. Aside from the religious and moral instruction it contains, the Bible is a repository of stories illustrating the forging of the Jewish identity. Tales of slavery, of conquest, of war, of defeat, and of loss illustrate emphatically that the Jewish nation has always been and always will be a Nation—with or without possession of its homeland.

Since the biblical dispersal of the ten tribes of Israel, the character of the Jewish people has been defined by its ability to survive. Long before the Jews withstood the Nazi holocaust of World War II, they endured the Babylonian exile, the Roman occupation, the Egyptian enslavement, the darkness of the Middle Ages, the persecution and torture of the Spanish Inquisition, the tyranny of the Crusades, and the failure of the Enlightenment to eradicate anti-Semitism. Homeless, mistrusted, feared, forced to die for their beliefs, losing touch with their Jewish past through assimilation and conversion, the national identity of the Jewish people has always remained, finally, inviolable.

Benjamin Disraeli put it most eloquently when he wrote, quite simply: "It is impossible to destroy the Jews."

Ancient Roots

The region where the land of Israel eventually emerged was once considered the center of the world. Situated at the confluence of three continents—Asia, Europe, and Africa—it was also geographically the locus, over the centuries,

of three great monotheistic religions: Judaism, Christianity, and Islam. The Middle East is the site of some of the most ancient civilizations. Jericho, located in the Jordan Valley, is considered the world's oldest known city, with fortifications that date back 9,000 years. Evidence of other early civilizations has also been found along the Mediterranean, in the

The Old City of Jerusalem, built by the Roman Emperor Hadrian in 135 C.E., is surrounded by a Medieval fortress of stone walls that enclose narrow, winding stone streets and walkways. Along the tops of the fortress walls are narrow catwalks upon which soldiers have tread for centuries, defending the city from invaders.

Negev, and on the hills of Judea. The Hebrews, as the Jews were first known, settled in the region roughly 6,000 years ago, primarily in the lands of southern Mesopotamia (modern Iraq), and eventually began migrating south to the Jordan valley, to the land of Galilee, and the Mediterranean coastal region that is today the domain of the modern state of Israel.

Sometime during the third millennium B.C.E. the region became largely occupied by tribes of Canaanites, a nomadic people who established small city-kingdoms along a strip of land between two very large and powerful nations, Egypt and Assyria. The land of Canaan, located along the roads that linked these two great nations, was often the site of intense battles between Egypt and Assyria.

Also at this time, there were many immigrants to the area from surrounding regions such as Mesopotamia, Asia Minor, and the Greek Islands—from which came the Philistines. According to legend, among these new immigrant groups was a man from the land of Ur, a Sumerian city in southern Mesopotamia, who was the leader of a small but culturally advanced tribe (the Bible says he had 318 trained servants born in his house) that some scholars believe was a tribe of Amorites. At the end of the third millennium B.C.E., scholars believe, this man, Abraham, crossed the desert with his people and set up camp in the land of Canaan, in a town called Beersheba.

The only record of the emergence of the Israelites as an organized nation comes from the Bible, where Abraham is recorded as the patriarch, the father of Judaism, and a descendent of Noah. The first recorded acquisition of land by the Jews is found in Chapter 23 of the Book of Genesis, which records that Abraham, following the death of his wife Sarah, purchased the Cave of Machpelah and the lands surrounding it as a burial place for her. It is a commonly held belief today that Abraham, who is considered to be the first Jew because he was the first to recognize the existence of a single, all-powerful God, is buried in this Cave, along with his wife, his son Isaac; and his grandson Jacob. The earliest teachings of the Jewish faith are based on the spiritual discoveries made by Abraham, Isaac, and Jacob in the city of Hebron, twenty miles south of Jerusalem, some 4,000 years ago.

According to the Bible, Jacob, the son of Isaac and the grandson of Abraham, adopted the name Israel following a night-long struggle with an angel, and from that time forward his people were known as the children or nation of Israel. The twelve tribes of Israel began with his twelve children.

The Book of Genesis provides the only recorded evidence that Abraham and his family ever existed. The first five books of the Old Testament are largely considered an ancient written record of an even older oral history that was passed down among the Hebrew tribes. In fact it is interesting to note that many details of the more fantastic, legendary elements of the first five books of the Bible—such as the great flood and the story of Noah's Ark—are also found in the writings of the Sumerian civilization, which is considered as old or older than the history recorded in the Old Testament.

It is possible that Abraham's wanderings were as much a result of economic as spiritual searching. "To your descendants I give this land from the river of Egypt to the great river," God tells Abraham, according to the Bible, "the river Euphrates, the land of the Kenites, the Kenizzites, the Kadmonites, the Hittites, the Perizzites, the Rephaim, the Amorites, the Canaanites, the Girgashites and the Jebusites." This is a description of the promised land, the notion of which is unique to the Israelite religion. The earliest books of the Bible are devoted to these central ideas: the Law handed down by God, the promise of the land and its fulfillment.

Jacob, the grandson of Abraham, is recorded as the founder of the twelve tribes of Israel. Indeed, according to the Bible the Nation of Israel was born when Jacob, following a nightlong struggle with an angel, was divinely renamed Israel. The meaning of the word *Israel* has been variously defined by scholars as "he who fights God," "he who fights for God," "he whom God fights," and "he whom God rules." Since the passage of the Bible where this story is first told is possibly one of the most mysterious and obscure within its pages, it has been a subject for much discussion over the centuries. Nevertheless the Bible's remaining record of Jacob's life and deeds shows that he is responsible for the founding of the idea of a race of people who define themselves as Jews.

The nation of Israel became a race distinct from any other (the word Hebrew, a largely pejorative derivative of the word *habiru* and used to describe the wandering tribes of Abraham's generation, was not descriptive enough since it included habiru tribes who were not followers of the Jewish law) and was personified in Jacob, who became known as Jacob Israel. The twelve tribes are said to be descended from him and his sons: Reuben, Simeon (Levi), Judah, Issachar, Zebulun, Benjamin, Dan, Naphtali, Gad, Asher, Ephraim, and Manasseh. Jacob and his sons are also credited with the successful conquest of the town of Shechem, the place where Abraham first made his covenant with God, and the Book of Genesis records an Israelite presence there even during their enslavement by the Egyptians. Shechem, described by the Jewish historian Josephus in 90 C.E. as being near the city of Neapolis near Jacob's Well, was the first continuous homeland for the Jews: the original central shrine and capital of Israelite Canaan.

After the Jewish slaves were freed by the Egyptian pharaoh Merneptah, they were led out of bondage by Moses, who took his people to the foot of Mount Sinai. From there he climbed to the mountaintop and received the revelations from God that were to be the moral foundation of the Jewish faith, including the Ten Commandments. While scholars dispute whether today's Mount Sinai is the same site to which Moses migrated during the Exodus of the Jews, this place remains to this day a focal point for pilgrims seeking holy revelation.

Based on biblical and archeological evidence, there is no doubt that West Semites migrated to Egypt in the third millennium B.C.E., first penetrating the Nile Delta. Many of these immigrants were seeking work or trade, though some were slaves, and many of these were tribes of habiru. There is no doubt that some of these habiru were related to the tribes of Abraham. Indeed, even after settling in the Lands of Canaan and in Shechem, there is evidence that some of Abraham's people continued their nomadic ways.

In the last quarter of the second millennium, the enslaved Israelites were driven to throw off their shackles and escape. The Egyptian king Rameses II (1304–1237 B.C.E.) ruled firmly over his subjects and employed vast numbers of slave laborers in the construction of tremendous buildings, the likes of which had not been seen since the original construction of the pyramids. Rameses' iron rule provoked a growing discontent among the Jews that manifested itself during the reign of the next Egyptian leader, Merneptah. The first reference to Israelis outside the territory of Egypt (a description of a battle with Israel, in a region described as beyond Sinai, in Canaan) occurs during his reign; this evidence of an Exodus comes from an Egyptian account, one of the earliest records of Israel from a nonbiblical source. The existence of such records gives credibility to the biblical stories of Moses and the Exodus from bondage.

The Jews fleeing Egypt knew they had a homeland to go to—knew that their people were waiting for them in Canaan. It is arguable that the Israelites who wandered with Moses in the desert for forty years were not the entire nation of Israel but a part of it. Yet the importance of the story lies not in whether it was the entire nation in exile or a part, but in the fact that before their enslavement by the Egyptians the Israelites were distinguished by a belief in a promise of greatness, in a covenant with a singular God, with whose help they had resisted the greatest empire then known to man. They emerged from slavery, and from wandering, a unified race of people. They also emerged with something that was to prove crucial to their survival: the Mosaic code, the core of which is known as the Ten Commandments—a set of written laws governing all aspects of daily life and ritual.

James J. Tissot (1836-1902) depicts a scene from Exodus in the Old Testament in his painting Moses Destroyeth the Tables of the Ten Commandments. When Moses descended from the top of Mount Sinai with God's precious gift to his people, he found that they had succumbed to superstition and fear, and constructed a golden calf to worship—even though this was in direct opposition to God's Law. In his rage at his people's faithlessness, Moses smashed the tablets upon which God had placed his Law.

Upon their return to Shechem, the Israelites took up residence there, and settled also in the areas east of the Jordan river, along the Jordan Valley, and in the mountains, while the Mediterranean coastal plain remained the home of the Philistines (though over the next two centuries the Israelites would conquer and settle the coast as well). At this point in their development, the Jews wandered less in search of commerce and conquest (or escape) and favored instead a more rooted farming and craft-oriented economy. This was a period of expansion and conflict, as the Israelites settled larger parts of the region that had previously been farmed and civilized by other peoples. As God tells them in the Book of Joshua: "I have given you a land for which ye did not labor, and cities which ye built not, and ye dwell in them; of the vineyards and oliveyards which ye planted not do ye eat."

So the Israelites settled the land of Canaan (sometimes taking lands from the Canaanites), free at last from slavery and loosely joined together as a nation, unified in at least one regard: the laws of God. Their system of government was tribal, and the settlement of disputes was left to judges. Though this was an essentially democratic and meritocratic society, its tribal nature was ultimately too disunited to be satisfactory. Nevertheless this system remained in effect until the nation's expansion put them in direct confrontation with the Philistines, a far more formidable enemy than the Canaanites.

In battling the Philistines for control of the Mediterranean coast, the Israelite nation evolved from an essentially theocratic to a monocratic form of government. Though at first reluctant to follow a king, the people sought and accepted the guidance and wisdom of their greatest prophet, Samuel, who was extremely wise. He selected a Benjaminite guerrilla fighter named Saul to lead the people of Israel. In accepting Saul as their first king and leader against the Philistines, the Israelites found unity, at least for a considerable period of time.

In the Book of Judges there is frequent reference to several lost histories that chronicle this period: The Book of the Chronicles of the Kings of Israel; The Books of the Chronicles of the Kings of Judah; and The Book of the Acts of Solomon, among others. Among the surviving records, including two books of Solomon and two of Kings, there is evidence of a rich and complex society showing, in some cases, exact dates for notable events such as the death of Saul (1005 B.C.E.), the reign of King David (until 966 B.C.E.), and the death of Solomon (926 or 925 B.C.). The Book of Judges and other extant records show that Saul was a dynamic if sometimes brutal and erratic military leader. As administrator he laid the groundwork for an Israeli monarchy, and did much to help unify the tribes. However, it was his successor, King David, who eventually delivered the promise of the monarchy and of the promised land.

At once fearsome, warlike, wise, and pious, David was the first King of Israel to secure the city of Jerusalem as his nation's capital. His roots as a warrior and a leader of soldiers, as depicted in this page from a Byzantine illuminated manuscript, combined with his genuine religious faith, made him an effective leader of his people. Forever after his conquest of Jerusalem, the site became known informally as the City of David.

Jerusalem, O Jerusalem

A brilliant statesman and ruler, David ascended the throne in 1000 B.C.E. It was King David (the same David who at one time killed Goliath with his slingshot) who finally defeated the Philistines and gained access to the Mediterranean. He also extended his realm to the east, north (as far as Damascus and the Euphrates River), and south (as far as the Red Sea). Gaining control, as well, of the highways that traversed the narrow strip of land that had once been home to the Canaanites, King David made a mighty and prosperous nation of the Israelites. This success was at least partly a matter of good fortune, for the Egyptian empire to the south had diminished considerably since the days of Moses, while those to the east, Assyria and Babylon, had yet to realize their full power. Still, it was David's breadth of knowledge, travels, and broad world-view that allowed Israel to flourish.

David's greatest achievement was the conquest of Jerusalem (until then the domain of the Canaanites), which had eluded capture for two hundred years. David claimed Jerusalem as his capital. This alone was considered a wise move, for the city of Jerusalem was centrally located among, yet neutrally positioned outside, the territories of the twelve tribes of Israel. Under the reign of King David the Israelites grew more powerful and more unified. In forging a single, central focus for the Israelite's religious heart, in placing the Ark of the Covenant in the Citadel (called Zion), he changed the thinking of his people, from seeing the presence of God in the Ark alone, or in high places alone, to recognizing a connection between the Ark's presence in "Zion" and Jerusalem it-

Unlike his father, David, King Solomon reigned over the promised land without employing massive armies or waging wars. He was a diplomat when it came to international relations, and within his own empire many of his ruling methods resembled those of the pharaohs and leaders of other nations. Instituting levies, in the form of forced labor, King Solomon built numerous grand structures and mined the lands for goods to be traded by sea. Today King Solomon's mines (pictured above) remain a silent yet beautifully haunting testament to the hard work of long-dead laborers.

self. Though in fact David did succeed in making Jerusalem the spiritual and geographical center of Jewish faith and existence for many centuries to come, he was less effective ultimately in uniting the still fractious twelve tribes of Israel as one nation behind a single king.

Solomon, David's son, was the next King of Israel. King Solomon, who inherited a strong and prosperous country at some point in the tenth century B.C.E., was a very different man from his father. While David had been passionate, rash, willful, conscious of sin, God-fearing, Solomon was far more secular, a product of his times, almost heartless in his rule, far more a Near Eastern monarch than any other Jewish king before him. Solomon forged an alliance with Egypt (taking an Egyptian princess as one of his wives) and, most notably, completed the religious centralization of the Jewish faith in Jerusalem with the construction of the first great Temple of Jerusalem.

Though he was considered a wise king, Solomon made a number of mistakes in his domestic government (including heavy taxation and forced labor) that, upon his death, resulted in an uprising that left a rift in the kingdom. The twelve tribes of Israel now split apart—the ten comprising the Kingdom of Israel cleaving to the lands to the north; the two comprising the Kingdom of Judah, the tribes of Benjamin and Judah, forming the House of David and pursuing self-government in the lands to the south. For the next 200 years the two kingdoms remained neighbors, sometimes friendly and sometimes hostile, depending on economic conditions then prevailing.

But the struggle within the Kingdom of Israel, between adherence to a strict religious and moral code on the one hand, and the need, on the other hand, to conform to the non-Jewish world in which they lived, was too great. It created an unresolveable conflict that made for constant infighting. Eventually, though, the demise of the Kingdom of Israel came when it aligned itself with Aram-Damascus to the north in a war with Assyria. When that war was lost, these ten tribes of Israel were dispersed and assimilated into distant lands, the capital of Samaria was totally destroyed, and the city of Shechem disappeared completely.

This was the first great mass tragedy in Jewish history. When they took their last, forced journey into Assyria, the ten tribes of the Kingdom of Israel became known as the lost tribes of Israel. Those Samaritans who remained intermarried and were assimilated into Aramaic cultures—to the point of losing their language, their history, and their religion.

The southern kingdom, meanwhile, survived the siege of the Assyrian army by making a treaty with its more powerful neighbor. For a century and a half the Israelites coexisted, if a bit uneasily, with Assyria . It was during this time that the Israelites underwent a reformation of sorts, led by the prophet Isaiah, who is considered one of the most remarkable of the prophets. Isaiah turned the focus of the Israelites from a religion of cult, endless sacrifices, and priestly ceremonies (which is where the days of King Solomon had led them), to an ethical religion of the heart.

When the Assyrian Empire was replaced by the Babylonian, the Judahs—as the Israelites were now known, for the tribe of Judah—attempted to rebel. The rebellion was a dismal failure. Babylonian King Nebuchadnezzar and his armies invaded Jerusalem and destroyed the Temple in 586 B.C.E. Many Jews were sent into exile, particularly to Babylonia. Thus, as it is written in the Book of Lamentations: "By the waters of Babylon we sat down and wept when we remembered Zion." By this time the Jewish sense of homeland had been firmly established on that small strip of land between Syria and Egypt that had once been the land of Canaan. But once again the Jews were in exile.

By the third century B.C.E., the Jews of Jerusalem had come under Persian rule. By all accounts this was a period of benign foreign rule during which Jewish literature and worship within synagogues began to evolve. But around 332 B.C.E., when Alexander of Macedon invaded Persia, this relatively calm period ended. Alexander (depicted in stone above) was the first European invader of Asia. His conquests caused the lands inhabited by the Jews to be taken over first by the Ptolemies and later by the Seleucids, whose rule inspired terror in the hearts of the Jews.

As fate and history would have it, the Babylonian Empire was conquered by the Persians some forty years after the destruction of Jerusalem. The Persian leader, Cyrus the Great, decreed that all exiled peoples be permitted to return to their homelands. Thus it was that the Jews of Babylonia were permitted to return once more to Judah. There they rebuilt the walls and the Temple of Jerusalem, and lived in relative harmony as a small and obscure province of the Persian Empire, albeit surrounded by hostile neighbors, including the Samaritans to the north—descendants of what was left of the ten tribes following assimilation and intermarriage with other peoples. Although few written records of this period exist, there is some evidence that Jews were free to practice and pursue their religious beliefs under the Persians. Perhaps the lack of contemporary records is due to the fact that during this time the Old Testament, as it is known today, emerged. It was called the Book of the Laws of Moses, but it was a history of the Jews.

This period of relatively peaceful existence in the homeland came to an end in 332 B.C.E, when Alexander the Great led his armies to a decisive defeat of the Persian Empire and the small tribe of Judah found itself, for the next nine centuries, subject to Greco-Roman rule. While initially this led to greater autonomy and religious freedom, by the second century B.C.E a growing Hellenistic, non-Jewish population had arisen within the small kingdom, and the Jews were increasingly subjugated to a Syrian-based dynasty that sought to enforce Greek-influenced religious practices.

Beit Zur, the ruins of which are shown here, was a fortress of the Maccabees during their successful resistance and revolt against the Seleucid monarch Antiochus Epiphanes. The Maccabees, a group of Jewish warriors led by the sons of Mattathias, most prominently the son known as Judas Maccabee, are said to have received divine assistance in their struggle against Seleucid oppression when a small amount of oil meant to last only a day somehow made light for eight days. This tale is the source of the Jewish celebration of Hannukah.

Regardless of the actual causes, the result was the imposition of intolerable conditions for the Israelites in their own homeland. Once again the Jewish people found themselves in a position of rebellion and armed resistance. This was also the beginning of what would become a significant new element in Jewish history, that of the martyrdom of individuals standing for what they believe in (and dying for their beliefs) rather than fleeing. From 166 to 164 B.C.E. the Israelites fought against the Greeks and ultimately drove them out of Judea. This uprising was led by the legendary Maccabee brothers, who saw themselves as reliving the Book of Joshua and reclaiming the promised land for their people. Their efforts culminated in the Jewish recapture of Jerusalem in 164 B.C.E.

For the next century, with Jewish sovereignty restored, the Israelites began to rebuild the former splendor of Jerusalem. But by 63 B.C.E., with the Roman Empire strong and on the rise, a still fractious Jewish state fell easy prey to its powerful, advancing armies. The Kingdom of Judah was renamed Judea. Although the conquered kingdom was subject to the authority of the Syrian governor, the state nonetheless retained enough autonomy to have its own king.

The first great king of the Roman period was Herod the Great (37–4 B.C.E.), who was treated as a friend of Rome and rewarded with gifts of territory, including the land known as Transjordan. Herod was both a Jew and an anti-Jew, an upholder and benefactor of Greco-Roman civilization. He ruled over all of the historic lands of Israel and rebuilt the Temple in Jerusalem, making it one of the most imposing structures of its time, a structure far grander and more elaborate than anything built or envisioned by King Solomon.

It was Herod who turned Jerusalem into a kind of Jewish mecca—making it a grand stopping place, a fantastic destination for Jewish pilgrims to visit three times a year, at Passover, Shavuot (the Feast of Weeks), and Sukkot (the Feast of Tabernacles). He was a grand planner, but also a ruthless autocrat. Upon assuming the throne in 37 B.C.E., the first thing he did was execute forty-six leading members of the Sanhedrin (a committee of elders responsible for deciding religious-legal matters) who had sought to uphold Mosaic law in secular matters, effectively separating once and for all any connection between Temple and state.

In their great study of world history, Will and Ariel Durant wrote of the widespread belief in and hope for a messiah at this time, the numerous sightings and claimants recorded, the aura of anticipation under which people lived and hoped for deliverance. The messianic culture had its roots in the belief that King David had been anointed by God so that he and his descendants could rule over Israel until the end of time, exercising dominion over alien peoples.

The era commencing around 4 B.C.E., when Herod died, was unstable and remained so until 70 C.E. when the Romans invaded Jerusalem once again, tearing the great Temple down to the ground and effectively dispersing the citizens of Judea into the diaspora. This tumultuous period of roughly seventy-five years marked the rise of Christianity following the emergence of Jesus Christ

In Jerusalem, a city that has survived through centuries of war, conquest, destruction, and resurrection, a portion of the ancient wall surrounding the Old City is lit by floodlights. It was here, in the area of the Old City, that King David and King Solomon led their people out of the tribal infighting that had divided them and into nationhood.

from among the many thousands of false messiahs of the day. Jews do not recognize Jesus as the Messiah to this day.

At this point, the diaspora (Jews living outside Israel) had grown to some six million Jews, one million of them living in Egypt alone. In Alexandria, perhaps the world's greatest city after Rome, they formed a majority in two out of its five quarters. Though most of the diaspora Jews were thriving under the liberal Roman rule in the Mediterranean and Near East, many of them were looking for a way to keep their faith while abandoning some of the more rigorous daily dictates of the Mosaic law. Meanwhile, in the homeland, small factions of Zealots were committed to the belief that the promised land was destined to be ruled by the Jews. This, coupled with the general rise in messianic fervor, is further evidence of a general underlying unrest.

Conflicts between Greco-Roman culture and Jewish culture were on the rise and with these tensions came early evidence of anti-Semitism (although the word *anti-Semitism* was not coined until 1879), which had begun in the second century B.C.E., when the Jewish people became distinctly recognized as a monotheistic culture. The Jews were the other, the strangers, the practitioners of rituals and habits (like circumcision and the dietary laws) that held them apart from all others. Indeed, the revolt of the Jews of

Judea against the Roman Empire that began in 66 C.E. started not in Jerusalem for political reasons but in Caesarea, following the resolution of a lawsuit between Greeks and Jews which the Greeks won.

Once word of what would become known as the Great Revolt reached Rome, armies were sent in to Jerusalem led by Vespasian and his son Titus, future emperors of Rome. By 69 C.E. father and son had reconquered Judea, save Jerusalem and one or two small fortresses. A long and bitter siege of Jerusalem began, and the city became a target of battle from without and within, as the various sects fought among themselves. But in the summer of 70 C.E., Titus and his armies finally broke through and captured the city. The Temple was burned down and its sacred contents carried off to Rome. Those inhabitants of the city who did not flee were massacred, sold as slaves, or saved to die in the arenas of Caesarea, Antioch, and Rome. The Jews lost their homeland, and, more importantly, Jerusalem and the great Temple that had become their spiritual center was destroyed.

Leather sandals from the first century C.E. found on Masada might have been worn by a Jewish martyr who chose to die rather than give up her faith.

The only remaining stronghold was Masada, in the southern desert, whose inhabitants held out for three more years before committing suicide rather than succumbing to capture. For a time thereafter the Jews attempted to occupy Jerusalem, but with the fortress destroyed there were no walls to protect them. In 135 C.E. the last outpost of Jewish culture in the region, the tiny town of Betar just southwest of the capital, also was destroyed by the Romans.

The Dark Ages

It is a tribute to the genius of the leaders of the Jewish people that in 70 C.E., rather than lose their faith upon the loss of their homeland (and upon the deaths of so many of their people), the remainder of the Jewish people—a good portion of whom had been living for many decades in the diaspora, but many of whom were now living in the regions surrounding the former Jerusalem—shifted the focus of their faith from the great Temple to their local places of worship.

Wherever a Jewish community existed, there God existed. Wherever a Jewish place of worship was established, there God was established. His spirit, contained in the Ark of the Covenant once carried on the backs of the slaves who fled bondage in Egypt in the time of Moses, became moveable once more. For now Zion would be relegated to a memory for millions of Jews, a former home—a promised land lost. Though it would remain lost for many centuries, the Jewish identity would not be lost. Rather, it would be affirmed by the private and public acts of faith and daily ritual that so many had fought to preserve for so long.

Those Jews who were not ensconced within communities in Egypt, such as Alexandria, found themselves living in the lands of Palestine (for that is what the Romans now chose to call the region that had once belonged to the Philistines). In fact, from this point on, a large Jewish population continued to live in Palestine, settling mostly in the north of the country, in Galilee. Here they lived much as they had always lived, according to their own laws, though this often led them to confrontation with the Romans. When the Romans outlawed circumcision in 135 C.E., the final Jewish rebellion, the Bar-Kochba revolt, occurred.

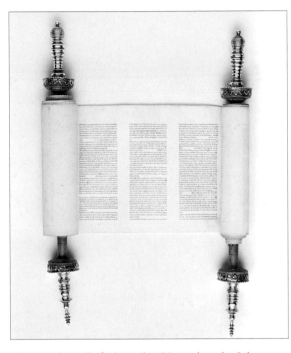

This Torah scroll, fashioned in Nuremberg by Johann Conrad Weiss circa 1700–1710, is written with ink on parchment, and hung on wood and silver rollers. The Torah consists of the Mosaic, the first five, books of the Old Testament. Also known as the Pentateuch, they began to emerge in written form during the time of the great prophet Samuel.

Following the uprising of 135 C.E.—as punishment for which the Jews' religious leaders were put to death—Jewish life was forced to become insular and private, when necessary practiced in secret. But the period of transition between 70 C.E. and 135 C.E. was long enough to complete the transformation of religious rites away from the focus on Jerusalem and the Temple and toward the Torah itself.

There is no doubt that this psychological and spiritual shift was to be the key to the survival of the Jewish people. The ensuing centuries were especially brutal for the Jews as both a people and a religion. At the time of Christ the world Jewish population was estimated at around eight million, including ten percent of the Roman Empire; by the tenth century C.E. that number had fallen to roughly one to one-and-a-half million Jews worldwide.

By the fourth century C.E., Christianity had so expanded throughout the Roman Empire that it was adopted as the state religion. Constantine the Great (288–377), the first Christian Emperor, proclaimed Palestine the Holy Land and caused churches and shrines to be erected throughout the region, especially in Jerusalem, Bethlehem, and Nazareth. Christian pilgrims flocked to Palestine, monasteries arose, and by the fifth century there was a Christian majority in the region. Though at all times Jews remained a presence in what had once been their homeland, their numbers remained small, and were to continue to remain small for the next twelve centuries.

As Christianity became firmly entrenched in the Roman Empire (and paganism virtually abolished), the Jews became conspicuous as a large, well-organized, comparatively wealthy, highly educated, religious minority who rejected Christianity on principle (rather than out of ignorance). During the late fourth and fifth centuries, Jews living in Christian cities found most of their communal rights and all of their privileges withdrawn. For the Jews these, indeed, were the beginning of the Dark Ages.

Meanwhile, to the east, another monotheistic religion having its basis in Judaism was growing: Islam. Arab records show

Mohammed stands before Mecca with the two symbols of his faith: the sword and the Book of the Koran. The Koran's story of Mohammed's journey upon a fabulous winged horse to the "furthermost place," where he came face to face with God and was given the teachings of Islam, is traditionally recognized as having taken place in Jerusalem at the site of the Dome of the Rock, now considered one of the most holy sites of Islam.

that as early as the first century B.C.E. (and possibly as early as the time of King David, or, even earlier, Moses), Judaism was spreading fast in northern Arabia, with some tribes becoming wholly Jewish. There is also evidence of as many as twenty Jewish tribes living in and around the region of Medina in the fourth century C.E., and it is even possible that a Jewish-governed state existed there at that time.

Here the form of Judaism practiced was more rigorous, no doubt an outcome of the preaching of extremist Essene sects at the desert fringes. This extreme asceticism, in the form of an uncompromising monotheism, attracted Mohammed and formed the basis for his religion, Islam. But when his early attempts to convert the desert Jews to his faith were rebuffed, Mohammed appears to have diverged from Judaism, thereafter giving Islam a deliberately new thrust that continued its development with a dogmatic dynamism all its own.

During the first dozen centuries of the common era the most fortunate Jews lived in Babylonia, under the leadership of princes (called exilarchs) with the claim of a direct descendancy from the House of King David and the kings of Judah. For a time Babylon became the center of Jewish life. It was here that the Babylonian Talmud, the most authoritative legal book developed by the Jews—one which would guide them for centuries to come—was written. Babylonian Jews were prominent in areas of learning and in the courts, as well as in agriculture, commerce, shipbuilding, and sailing. Though the power of the exilarchs to rule the lives of their own people began to decline in the third century, with the rise of the Sassanid dynasty and the Zoroastrian faith, the Babylonian Jewish community managed to survive for many centuries.

During the seventh century the Arabs invaded Palestine and installed Islamic temples and peoples there. Jerusalem now became a holy Muslim city. The great Dome of the Rock (or Mosque of Omar) was constructed atop the ruins of the Jewish Temple (above the Wailing Wall) in 691. The city of Jerusalem was now the sacred home to three great monotheistic faiths: Christianity, Islam, and Judaism. The seat of Christianity, meanwhile removed to Rome, saw the domination of the Holy Land by Islam as a sacrilege. So it was that in 1095 the Pope decreed and blessed the first of a series of what were to become known as the Crusades, aimed at the armed recovery of the Holy Land in the name of Christianity.

By 1099 the Crusaders succeeded in reclaiming most of the Holy Land, in the process slaughtering many of the region's Muslim and Jewish inhabitants. The Kingdom of Jerusalem, as they dubbed the city, then became the capital of the Holy Roman Empire, which lasted for two centuries, until 1291, when the Europeans were driven out by the Egyptians.

During the period of the Holy Roman Empire, Jews traveled great distances in pursuit of religious freedom, forming colonies throughout the Mediterranean, as far north as Lyons, Bonn, and Cologne, and as far west as Cadiz and Toledo. During the Dark Ages they traveled even further north and east, as far as the Baltics, Poland, and the Ukraine. Though part of the reason for the dwindling numbers of Jews can be attributed to war, economics, and other demographic factors, a large contributing factor during this period was the effect of assimilation and a general blending in to the local populations.

The land of Israel, after centuries of conquest, division, and reunion, has become home to many faiths. Baha'i, a world religion which developed out of a mystical Islamic movement around 1850, has its world center, the glistening dome of which can be seen above the harbor, in Haifa. The grave of Baha'Allah, for whom the movement is named, is found in nearby Akko.

Though their numbers remained small, the Jews played an important role in the growth of Europe during the Dark Ages. As they migrated away from Palestine, they moved toward the towns and cities that began to spring up in Europe, often bringing with them urban skills learned in the cities of antiquity. Following the almost total destruction of Palestinian Jews in the second century C.E., the people of Israel turned from the rural lifestyle to which they were accustomed and adapted to the demands of city life. The Jews, in short, became city dwellers as a matter of necessity. Driven out of their homeland and the business of an agricultural society, they survived by learning the skills of craftsmen, tradesmen, and dealers. Thus by an accident of circumstance, the Jews became a crucial link between the cities of Roman antiquity and the emerging town communes of the Middle Ages.

To the east the Jews also settled in the Arab-Moslem territories that included, in the early Middle Ages, Spain, North Africa, and the Near East south of Anatolia. In the Moslem regions the Jews by and large fared well, though they refused to acknowledge the prophetic mission of Mohammed (just as they refused to recognize Jesus Christ). Though Mohammed was not any more accepting of Judaism than it was of him, and ultimately massacred the Jews of Medina, he did evolve a system whereby the two cultures could coexist.

The Jews, who supplied Moslem courts with a steady stream of doctors, astronomers, and officials over the centuries, in addition to offering a reliable and steady source of tax income under the principles of dhimma (which refers to Mohammed's strategy for the coexistence of Jews and Arabs), proved especially useful during the Arab years of conquest. In particular the Jews came to the aid of their rulers during the Moslem conquest of Spain that began in 711. In fact, between the eighth and eleventh centuries the most successful area of Jewish settlement was Spain, where two distinct communities of Jews thrived: those linked with the academies of Babylon and those who migrated from Palestine.

In the Middle Ages in Europe, Jews plied a variety of trades, but gradually they were limited, by law and out of practical necessity, to being moneylenders and bankers, in an association that ultimately led to negative stereotypes.

Early in the twelfth century, however, a new wave of Moslem fundamentalism in the Atlas Mountains of North Africa changed this heretofore relatively peaceful coexistence: Christians, some of whom had lived in the region for a thousand years, and Jews alike were given the choice of conversion to Islam or death. This fundamentalist shift soon moved into Spain where, beginning in 1146, the Jewish community was systematically shut down, its grand architecture developed over centuries destroyed. Jews were forced to wear identifying uniforms (of a humiliating quality) and routinely forced, at sword-point, to convert or die. Many Jews during this period pretended to convert (a similar conversion had been effected earlier under the reign of the Crusading Christians of Rome), resorting to secret worship of their God, though of course many simply converted. The end result was another period of migration for the Jews.

Meanwhile, following the collapse of the Holy Roman Empire in 1291, Palestine was governed by the Mamelukes, the slave-sultans of Egypt who had been imported from Asia for training as an elite military corps. For the two or three centuries following the demise of the Crusaders, the region was ruled by a military force loyal to Egypt. The only bright spot under the rule of the Mamelukes was that Jerusalem benefited from the construction of elaborate architecture, including parts of the old city of Jerusalem that remain standing to this day.

In 1516–1517 the Marmeluke Empire was defeated by the Ottoman Turkish Sultan Selim, following which the holy land came under Turkish rule for four centuries. Suleiman the Magnificent, Selim's son, ruled from 1520 to 1566, bringing prosperity back to the region, developing agriculture, and improving travel conditions. The magnificent walls that surround the city of Jerusalem today were constructed by Suleiman. By the seventeenth century, however, the Ottoman Empire was on the decline and conditions in the holy land deteriorated once more.

During the second half of the Middle Ages, the presence of the Jews in Europe and as far north as England became increasingly problematic in direct proportion to the cities' declining need for their particular talents with respect to crafts and trade. Early in the Middle Ages, the Jews had found themselves in the peculiar position of being free, by their own beliefs, to lend money to Christians (but not to each other), who themselves were banned from banking (from the handling of money) by the Christian faith. The result was that Jews became associated with banking and moneylending. As Europe matured and needed its Jews less, anti-Semitism rose; bizarre tales connected with the blood libel began circulating. The Jews became a target for clerical anti-Semitism.

In a steel engraving, a deputation of Jews cowers before King Ferdinand and Queen Isabella of Spain during the Inquisition as a priest tries to convert them to Catholicism. Many Jews pretended to convert but continued to practice their faith in secret, for which they were severely punished.

When the Black Death began spreading north to Europe from the Mediterranean, Jews were blamed. People accused Jews of poisoning wells, of spreading illness wherever they went. They were tortured into confessing that they were responsible for the plague (which killed one-fourth to one-half of the general population). Though Pope Clement VI issued a statement in 1248 pointing out that the Jews were suffering just as much as anyone else, and blaming the plague on the Devil, and though many other leaders issued similar defenses, Jews suffered the greatest wave of anti-Semitism since the first crusade in 1096.

Ironically it was in Spain, where the Jews had flourished for centuries, that they suffered some of the most organized, thorough, and systematic forms of clerical and nationalistic anti-Semitism. The Spanish Inquisition was spearheaded by a Dominican prior named Tomás de Torquemada, but it was created by King Ferdinand and Queen Isabella. Commencing in January 1481, over 700 heretics were burned at the stake in eight years (though some sources put the figure closer to 2,000). In less than twelve years, the Inquisition condemned more than 13,000 "conversos," or converts, for secretly practicing Judaism. During the entire period of the Inquisition, which lasted until 1834, more than 341,000 people were tried and found guilty of religious crimes: 32,000 were killed by burning, 17,659 were burned in effigy, and 291,000 were given lesser punishments. Most of the victims were Jews.

By the fourteenth century, the migrations and assimilations of the Jews had created two distinct groups: the Spanish or Sephardic Jews (the term is a corruption of an old Hebrew name for Spain) and the Ashkenazi or Germanic Jews. As a result of the Spanish Inquisition, the Sephardi began to migrate all over the Mediterranean and Moslem world, including to France, Portugal, and northwest Europe.

This new diaspora of Jews, however, took place at the end of the Middle Ages—a time when Europe no longer had much use for the skills of learning and craftsmanship that for centuries had been the Jews' admission ticket to all nations. After persecuting its converts for a dozen years, in 1492 the Spanish (in a neat twist of irony) then chose to exile all Jews who refused to convert to Christianity. This move followed similar expulsions of Jews from Vienna and Linz in 1421, Cologne in 1424, Augsburg in 1439, Bavaria in 1442 and 1450, Moravia in 1454, Perugia in 1489, Vicenza in 1486, Parma in 1488, Milan and Lucca in 1489, Florence and Tuscany in 1494, and Portugal in 1497. By the year 1500, the Jews were virtually eliminated from all large-scale trade and industry in Italy, Provence, and Germany. By then, Poland was considered the last safe place in Europe to be Jewish, and it soon became the heart of the Ashkenazi settlement, though there were expulsions and violence there, too.

A synagogue in what was at one time the Jewish ghetto of Rome is a testament to the thriving religious life of the Jews in the diaspora. As early as the first decades of the first century there were already 50,000 Jews living in Rome. Because they would not worship the gods of the Roman Empire, Jews were excluded from Roman religious festivals and from serving in the army.

Diaspora

Those refugees from Spain and Portugal who did not flee to the north found friendly settlements in Constantinople and Ottoman Salonika; the latter became one of the largest Jewish communities in the world, numbering 20,000 Jews in 1553. The sixteenth century also saw the development of the first Jewish "ghettos" in Italy.

But the Jews were not particularly safe among the Turks. Indeed, beginning in the fifteenth century and continuing for some 300 years, it was not uncommon for Jews to be taken hostage by Turks (often from Christian trading vessels, though they might just as likely be taken from Ottoman ships) and released only upon the payment of ransom. Jewish captives whose ransom was not paid were either killed or incarcerated in slave prisons. The practice appears to have thrived due to the fact that Jews were so willing and ready to pay for the freedom of their brethren.

During the sixteenth and seventeenth centuries, in fact, the abductions became so widespread that members of the Jewish community throughout Italy (who were most often at risk) made payments to a fund that acted as a kind of insurance guaranteeing payment of ransom should they be kidnapped. It was not just the Jews of Italy who maintained ransom funds. As late as 1748 the Jewish community of London is said to have paid £80 to obtain the release of a group of Jewish slaves in Malta. Napoleon brought an end to the practice of Jewish slavery thirty years later.

The Christian Reformation began in the sixteenth century, and with it arose a renewed interest by non-Jews in Hebrew and the Old Testament. During this period, though still confined to ghettos throughout Italy, the Jews to the north in countries where Protestantism took hold (like Britain, Holland, and the Baltics) fared well.

Even in Italy the Jews benefited for a time from the Reformation. For example, there was a rise in the number of Jewish texts published there, including the publication of the Talmud in 1520–1523 and, in 1574, a pocket edition of the book that is still in use today. During the latter half of the sixteenth century, however, the Counter-Reformation, spurred on by fear and mistrust of immigrants (of which group Jews were always a large part) and fear of the new religious ideas, prompted a new wave of anti-Semitism in Europe. It was during this time that more Jews traveled north to Britain and Holland.

Meanwhile, to the east, Jewish settlements along the Black Sea and the Russian border, which some believe dated back to the dispersion of the Ten Lost Tribes of the Kingdom of Israel, began to break up in the wake of Ivan the Terrible's decree that any Jew who failed to convert to Christianity would be drowned. Thus, Russian Jews began to migrate, seeking refuge in Poland, Lithuania, and the Ukraine. In 1500 there were only about 15,000 to 20,000 Jews in those regions, but by 1575 that number had multiplied to 150,000.

The Act Noy synagogue in Prague continues to serve a small Jewish community to this day. Jews in Prague suffered much persecution over the centuries, especially during the twelfth century, at the time of the Second Crusade, and during World War II. But during the sixteenth and seventeenth centuries, under the rules of the Holy Roman Emperor Maximilian II and his successor, Rudolph II, they managed to live in relative peace.

In 1503 the King of Poland named Rabbi Jacob Polak "Rabbi of Poland," and charged him with governing the Jews of Poland; by 1551 this position was elected by the Jews themselves. From 1560 onward, Jewish pioneers played a leading role in the economic development of Poland primarily, but also to a lesser degree Lithuania and the Ukraine, managing estates, leasing them in some cases, building and running mills and distilleries, running tolls, owning and operating river boats, trading goods, and manufacturing soap and furs. Entire villages inhabited by Jews, known as shtetls, arose during this period.

As the Counter-Reformation ended by the end of the sixteenth century, there emerged a new, enlightened approach to public policy that envisioned nations governed by secular rather than religious authority. Under these circumstances the Jews, especially those who were sophisticated and adept in the ways of commerce, began to thrive in Western and in Eastern Europe. In fact many countries started to relax their close scrutiny of Jewish settlers, especially in Holland, where from the 1620s on the Jews became a welcome addition to the mercantile community. From Holland, many Jews went west to the New World, to New York, where the first North American Jewish settlement was founded in 1654. This was also a period of Jewish settlement in South America, most notably Brazil and the Caribbean.

Shabbetai Zevi (1626-1676) was proclaimed the Messiah on May 31, 1665, by a resident of Gaza known as Nathan of Gaza (Abraham Nathan ben Elisha Hayyim Ashkenazi, 1643 - 1680). During the seventeenth century, Jews throughout Europe and Asia were only too eager to believe in a messiah. Thus, even after Zevi's conversion to Islam (which he chose over being put to death) and his later death, the Shabbetean movement continued for over a century.

In many German-speaking towns where Jews had been expelled earlier in the century they were now readmitted, including Bohemia, Vienna, and Prague. Rudolph II, the Hapsburg Emperor of the Holy Roman Empire, even gave the Jews a charter of privileges that included the right to construct a synagogue and the right to deny entrance therein to the police. The Hapsburgs in return earned the loyalty of the Jews to such an extent that by 1618, when the Thirty Years War broke out in Germany, they were instrumental in helping the Hapsburgs to maintain their power.

In 1648 in Poland, however, the Jews became the target of the Cossack rebellion against Polish rule and the Church. Thousands of Jews were murdered as they fled their shtetls for the seeming safety of large, fortified towns, only to be handed over by Polish troops to the murdering Cossacks in exchange for their own lives.

The Cossack rebellion took a huge emotional toll on the Jews. In response to the calamity, the more apocalyptic elements of Judaism took hold once again. The Jews of Poland turned to kabbalistic mysticism and the hope of a messianic deliverance from suffering.

These two threads of Judaism differed from the mysticism and messianism that produced Jesus Christ. For these two elements had been altered and entwined by two important events in recent Jewish history and culture: the rise of the Jewish press in the sixteenth century, which saw the publication of a version of the Zohar (a mystical, or kabbalistic, anthology) that included not only a guide to the mystical knowledge of God but also a healthy dose of ghetto folk-superstitions and the Haggadic tales of the people; and the evolution of the kabbalah itself during the Spanish exile, which added an element that connected the idea of Zion with the coming of the Messiah.

The Cossack rebellion of 1648, followed by the Swedish War of the late 1650s, coupled with a rising number of Jewish refugees in Europe in the 1660s, appeared to be signs of things to come. At the same time, in lands as far away from Poland as Morocco, Salonika, the Balkans, Turkey, Egypt, and Palestine, the teachings of Isaac ben Solomon Luria (known as The Lion) became more widespread. Luria was a sixteenth-century scholar whose philosophy united traditional Zohar practices and beliefs with the notion of angels, devils, and other folk mysticism of the age, including a profound messianism.

Thus when Nathan of Gaza (a clever but opportunistic scholar living in the Middle East) declared the Shabbetai Zevi (a man who was probably, at the very least, a manic depressive with delusions of greatness) the Messiah in 1665, the stage was set for Jews from Poland to Amsterdam to Constantinople to start packing their bags and heading for Jerusalem. Rich men sold all their worldly goods and set sail for the Holy Land, hoping to catch sight of the Messiah. Ultimately, though, Zevi was denounced by the Arabs as a fraud and converted to Islam rather than suffer execution. The Jewish taste for messianism was shattered, and Jewish officials in Jerusalem fell all over themselves declaring that they knew all along that Zevi had been a fraud.

Meanwhile, the Jewish migration to England in the mid-seventeenth century was taking on messianic proportions in its own right. In 1648, when the Polish massacre tipped off a renewed bout of Jewish migration into western Europe, the Jews of Amsterdam feared the effect that a large influx of refugees might have upon their already stable community (albeit without the rights of Dutch citizenship). This fear proved not to be farfetched, since a large stream of Jewish refugees into Hamburg in 1649 prompted a temporary expulsion of all Jews. Thus it was that the Jews found themselves looking further north for refuge, to England.

A Jewish New Year greeting card sent from Germany to New York in the early twentieth century. In the New World, Jews were allowed to observe their own holidays without persecution. The traditional holidays celebrated by Jews worldwide, including Rosh Hashanah (the Jewish New Year), Yom Kippur (the day of Atonement), and Passover (commemorating the liberation from Egypt), held the people together during the centuries of exile.

The year 1649 was a momentous year in England: it was the year of the defeat of English royalists and the execution of King Charles I. The political event offered Jews a unique opportunity for migration, as the Puritans who rose to power were sympathetic to a Semitic tradition; also, many of them believed in the Second Coming, which according to the Bible would not take place until the Jews had been dispersed to the ends of the earth. Moreover, the medieval Hebrew name for England, Kezeh ha-Arez, literally translated means "end of the earth." Here was the basis for fundamentalist agreement among Jews and Puritans.

Jews began to attain genuine citizenship in England under the Nonconformist Act of 1664, whereby citizenship was granted so long as they were willing to obey the laws of the land. This was the first time Jews had been granted full citizenship anywhere since their expulsion from Jerusalem in 70 C.E. As English citizens, Jews began to colonize America, where in 1665 the right to religious freedom was proclaimed by New York's first English governor.

In the New World, Jews enjoyed citizenship without religious barriers for the first time in the history of the diaspora. There was no imposition of any kind of special status to segregate them from other residents of the country. Even before the Declaration of Independence, American Jews found that they did not need to maintain a separate system of laws, except of course on matters that remained purely religious, which they were free to do in any event. The growth of American Jewry added a third element to the existing dualism of Eretz Yisrael, or Zion, and the diaspora. This third element would prove instrumental in the evolution of Zionism, which in turn made the rebirth of the state of Israel possible.

This 1962 lithograph by Anatole Kaplan is entitled Yiddish Folksongs: Play Me a Song of Peace. *Although Hebrew is both the language of the Torah and the official language of Israel, Yiddish has long been a part of Jewish culture. It began developing during the thirteenth century as migrating Jews came into contact with the German tongue. During the eighteenth and nineteenth centuries modern Yiddish spread as the numbers of Jews in Europe grew, leading to books, newspapers, theater, and songs in Yiddish.*

By the start of the eighteenth century, the Age of Enlightenment was underway. People were no longer willing to die for their religious beliefs, at least at the top of society. At the other levels of society it was another story altogether, as evidenced by the Pietist movement in Germany, the Methodist movement in England, the Great Awakening in America, and the rise of Hasidism in Eastern Europe, where half of all Jews now lived.

Hasidism, with its devotion to ecstasy, miracles, and visions, appeared to be an extension of the Shabbatean spirit of the late seventeenth century, a development of the Lurian teachings that favored folk mysticism and kabbalah. One of the many changes wrought by the Hasidic movement was that Jews began to shun the synagogue for prayer houses of their own creation—the natural extension of the original movement away from the Great Temple of Jerusalem. If any temple could become home to the Ark of the Covenant, it followed that poor Jews could designate any house a house of worship too. The Hasidim also prayed differently than the establishment Jews: loudly, with a great deal of singing and dancing.

Once again there was to be a serious rift in the Jewish community, with some orthodox scholars going so far as to advocate persecution of the Hasidim. Ultimately Hasidism spread into Germany, and from there throughout the world, and the orthodox attempt to stamp it out failed.

Russia, meanwhile, which had until the eighteenth century effectively barred most Jews from settling within its borders, found itself acquiring some 1 million Jewish citizens with its partitions of Poland in 1772, 1793, and 1795. Thus saddled with a nation of Jews, Russia gave them rights of residence, but only within a Pale of Settlement—a ghetto where their numbers and problems increased rapidly.

In Europe, the Enlightenment would prove to be equally unkind to the Jews. In Italy, the anti-Semitic Pope Pius VI (1775–1799) published an Edict on Jews early in his reign that led to forced baptisms, among other insults to their faith. In Prague, the Jews were expelled in 1744–1745, though readmitted three years later. In 1750 Prussian King Frederick the Great imposed a law that distinguished between "ordinary" and "extraordinary" Jews. Throughout Europe there were Jew Reforms and Edicts of Toleration with respect to the Jews, all of which gave some freedoms while taking others away.

The French Revolution in 1789, which in theory had as its goal the granting of all rights to all men (including Jews), presented an opportunity to argue the Jewish Question. The issue: how to recognize the rights of individual Jews without creating a nation of Jews (with rights) within the nation of France. Though after bitter debate it was ultimately decided that the Jews would be recognized as individuals (but not as a nation) and given rights of citizenship, that did not change the deeply held feelings of anti-Semitism that prompted the French Assembly to give the government the right to supervise debts owed to Jews in eastern France.

Jews became free citizens within Revolutionary France, and that freedom began to spread as the revolution spread. Jews were recognized as citizens in the Netherlands in 1796. In 1796–1798, Napoleon Bonaparte liberated the Jews of Italy. In 1812 Prussia recognized Jews already resident there as full citizens, abolishing all special taxes and disabilities.

Alfred Dreyfus (1859-1935), a French military officer, was a French-born man of Jewish descent accused of espionage and tried in the French courts in 1894. Although there was no proof against him, Dreyfus was sentenced to life in prison. He was publicly humiliated and sent to live on Devil's Island, the only inhabitant there save his guards. His case became a cause célèbre in turn-of-the-century France, in part because he appeared to have been convicted primarily because he was Jew, and in part because new evidence eventually surfaced implicating another man.

For nearly a century, until their faith in France was shattered by the Dreyfus case, the Jews were to look to the French as the nation that had done more for them than any other in Europe. But the seeds for the secular anti-Semitism had already been sown by the writings of Voltaire, Diderot, and Baron D'Holbach, among others. When the Jews were emancipated by the revolution, they soon found themselves borne into the heart of modern anti-Semitism, on the one hand accused of being, by virtue of their beliefs, obscurantists opposed to progress, and on the other hand condemned as the allies and instigators of anarchy.

The eighteenth-century Enlightenment evolved into the nineteenth century Industrial Revolution, during which time some very wealthy and powerful Jewish fortunes were made in Europe, including those of the Rothschilds, the Oppenheims, and the Mendelssohns, to name a few. This was also to be the century of Benjamin Disraeli, the most powerful British statesmen of Jewish descent (Disraeli was born in England in 1805 and baptized into the Anglican Church in 1817).

Perhaps not uncoincidentally, the nineteenth century saw the emergence of a reformation of Judaism (a first in all the centuries of exile), the result of which was the virtual elimination of the messianic elements of the past as well as the removal of all references to a return to the holy land. In 1819, in Hamburg, Jewish worship practices were reformed in the spirit of Luther's reformation of the church. Indeed, reform Judaism was primarily a German-driven phenomenon, in contrast to the thriving Hasidism of Eastern European Jewry.

This oil painting, executed by Minkowski circa 1910, is entitled After the Pogrom. *The images of homeless, forlorn women and children are a chilling reminder of the history of the Jews in the diaspora, a history of persecution and exile.*

During the period 1800–1880, the make-up of the Jewish population throughout the world saw a rise in the number of Ashkenazi, or European, as opposed to Sephardic, or Mediterranean, Jews. In the Afro-Asian Mediterranean, where most of the Sephardic Jews resided at this time, there were roughly 500,000 to 750,000 Jews; in Europe, by contrast, there were some 2 to 7 million Jews, mostly Ashkenazi. The Jewish community, in fact, grew enormously in the nineteenth century. Whereas in 1800 it was unusual to come across a city with more than 10,000 Jews, by 1880 Warsaw had 125,000 Jews, while in Vienna, Budapest, Odessa, and Berlin, the Jewish population was as high as 50,000. New York City also boasted a Jewish population of around 50,000 at this time; from the end of the nineteenth century onward, in fact, the United States would become the chief destination for Jewish immigrants.

Anti-Semitism remained virile in Western and Eastern Europe in the nineteenth century. In Tsarist Russia, in particular, anti-Semitism remained a part of codified law; Jews were forced to live within the Pale of Settlement and to carry identity cards that labeled them as Jews.

In 1871 the first modern Russian pogrom, instigated primarily by Greek merchants, took place in Odessa. By 1881, pogroms were a state-run event designed to rid Russia of its Jews. Like the Spanish expulsion of Jews in 1492, 1881 marked a new Jewish flight—this time west from Russia. From that year onward some 50,000 Jews fled the region annually; 110,000 Jews fled Moscow in 1891; another 137,000 left the country in 1892. In 1905–1906, 200,000 Jews emigrated out of Eastern Europe. Then, as with the cumulative effect of the exodus from Spain, Jewish emigration began to spread. Between 1881 and 1914, 350,000 Jews left Austrian Galicia. Roughly 2.5 million Jews emigrated from Eastern Europe during this period, most of them to America. Nevertheless, the Jewish population in Eastern Europe remained strong, numbering 5.5 million in 1914.

Zion

While history is certainly the sum of many millions of tiny events (and historical accounts simply a selective rendering of certain moments), in the story of any nation there is always a handful of people and events that seem to define the course of history. Thus it is that the State of Israel would not have been born in 1948 were it not for all the centuries of Jewish exile, were it not for all the centuries of persecution, and, above all, were it not for the strength of Jewish faith and identity. There were several crucial people and events in the nineteenth and early twentieth centuries without which Israel would not exist today.

The end of the nineteenth century was a unique moment in Jewish history. On the one hand, it was a time when more Jews than ever were assimilating into the cultures of Europe, Asia, and the United States, a time when the faith itself was being reformed to suit that assimilation, when Jews were enjoying more emancipation than ever. On the other hand, they faced as much persecution as ever.

Jews could easily have continued their centuries-old pattern of migration and assimilation, which by now was beginning to erode some of the most essential tenets of Judaism (a belief that Israel was the promised land, a belief that the Jews belonged there, a belief that a return to the promised land was the highest goal of the people after the worship of God). If this erosion was to be stopped, then something was needed to galvanize the Jewish people, to reinvigorate their faith in the reestablishment of a homeland.

The Jews needed to come to a rallying point on the issue of nationalism. As intellectual and religious thinking evolved away from the fantastic, mystical notion of a messiah who would deliver them, and as the modern separation grew between state and commerce, on the one hand, and faith and culture, on the other, there seemed to be only one means to that end: the rational, methodical, and political negotiation of a new homeland.

Dr. Theodor Herzl founded the Zionist movement in France in January 1895, on the day that he saw Alfred Dreyfus publicly humiliated before crowds of Parisians shouting "Death to the Jews!" Herzl, who was in town covering the trial for a Viennese newspaper, was so appalled at this spectacle of anti-Semitism that he set out to write a novel to express his outrage, and somehow ended up writing a recipe for Jewish statehood and independence that was to become known as Zionism.

The idea of a return to a holy land needed to capture the imagination of the people before a pilgrimage to Israel had any hope of beginning. What the Jews needed, in short, was Zionism. How they got what they needed can be told in the story of the life of one man, a visionary with the nerve and ability not just to conceive of a modern Zionist movement, but the intelligence and strength to launch it and follow it through until his death. That visionary was Theodor Herzl (1860–1904).

Herzl himself was the product of a nationalist movement that was tipped off by two seminal events in the history of anti-Semitism: the first, in 1839–40, took place in Damascus, where following the death of a Capuchin friar the Jews living there were accused of ritual murder and the blood libel, and were victims of riots, imprisonment, and torture on a massive scale; the second, in 1881, took place when Tsar Alexander II was assassinated by a revolutionary's bomb. Russia, swept by unrest and anti-Jewish sentiment—which had always been encouraged by the government—erupted in riots and pogroms aimed directly at the scapegoats.

The Damascus Gate in Jerusalem, the northern entrance to the Old City around 1903. The gate's tapered carved-stone crenellations and ornamented embrasures are the most beautiful example of the sixteenth century city walls. The Damascus gate is the busiest of the seven gates of Jerusalem that are still in use. Today it is the main connection between the Old City and the Arab communities of East Jerusalem.

Jewish intellectuals throughout Europe were profoundly affected by the violence of both the 1839 and the 1881 pogroms, and a movement toward Jewish nationalism developed from their awareness of a need for action. A German Jewish socialist named Moses Hess was so profoundly affected by the violence in Damascus that he saw, for the first time, that no matter how assimilated he might become, he would always be perceived as a Jew—and that as long as Jews remained homeless they would have no refuge from blind hatred. In 1862, Hess published *Rome and Jerusalem: The Latest National Question*, in which he declared that the time had come "for resettlement on the banks of Jordan."

Variations on the same theme would be heard throughout the nineteenth century, growing louder and more vigorous with the 1881 incidents in Russia. In Prussia, in 1860, Rabbi Hirsch Kalischer wrote: "Let no one imagine that the Redemption of Israel and the Messiah will suddenly appear from heaven and that amid miracles and wonders he will gather the Israelites of the Diaspora to their ancient inheritance. The beginning of the Redemption will take place in a natural way by the desire of the Jews to settle in Palestine and the willingness of the nations to help them in their work."

That same year, 1860, the Alliance Universelle Israelite, a philanthropic organization dedicated to the salvation of persecuted Jews worldwide through their resettlement in Palestine, was founded in Paris. In 1870, the Alliance set up an agricultural training school in Jaffa. Indeed, toward the end of the nineteenth century there were several societies in Russia and the United States whose mission was to encourage Jewish emigration to Turkish-controlled Palestine. These societies, called Hovevi Zion (Lovers of Zion), formed affiliated groups in Europe and actually founded several small settlements in Palestine.

When the 1881 massacres in Russia were followed in 1882 by the May Laws, which were designed to make Jewish life in Russia impossible, all this talk of statehood began to have deeper meaning. In 1882, a doctor named Leon Pinsker published a tract entitled "Autoemanzipation," which advocated that Jews buy themselves safety from persecution in a homeland, be it Palestine or anywhere else. By 1890, the term *Zionism* was officially coined by the socialist Nathan Birnbaum, primarily for use as a call to political action, a catchphrase meant to inspire Jews toward the creation of a Jewish state.

Even among non-Jewish writers the issue of Jewish nationalism was beginning to take hold. In England, which was to play a crucial role in the formation of the state of Israel, writers such as George Eliot agitated for greater awareness of the issue.

The tide was rising in favor of Jewish nationalism. In 1894, the Dreyfus Affair caught the attention of Europe when Captain Alfred Dreyfus, a Jewish officer on the French General Staff, was accused of being a German spy and France revealed its deep-seated anti-Semitism to the world. Herzl, who had been the Paris correspondent for the *Neue Freie Presse* of Vienna during the trial, was inflamed by the spectacle of hatred the trial unleashed. While covering the trial for the paper, he witnessed the French mobs' cries of "A mort! A mort les Juifs!" ("Death to the Jews!")

It shocked him, literally, into action: "Until that time most of us believed that the solution of the Jewish question was to be patiently waited for as part of the general development of mankind. But when a people, which in every other respect is so progressive and so highly civilized, can take such a turn, what are we to expect from other peoples, which have not even attained the level France attained a hundred years ago?" He reported in his diaries that from that moment on he became gripped by a sense of destiny.

Baron Edmond de Rothschild (1845-1934) was a member of the French branch of the powerful Rothschild banking family, and his financial help was instrumental in making Jewish colonization of Palestine happen. Following a visit to Palestine in 1914, Rothschild told Dr. Chaim Weizmann: "Without me the Zionists could have done nothing, but without the Zionists my work would have been dead."

Then Herzl wrote his seminal pamphlet, "Der Judenstaat," originally called "Address to the Rothschilds," in which he outlined a distinctive plan for the establishment of a Jewish nation. At first there was little response to "Judenstaat." His newspaper would not publish the tract, which he read aloud to friends, including a member of the Rothschild family. Then, as luck would have it, he was invited to speak at the Maccabean Society in London, where he was to find his first sympathetic and enthusiastic listeners. This led to a request that he contribute an article to the *Jewish Chronicle*, a highly respected English newspaper. He thereupon produced a condensed version of "Judenstaat," which the *Chronicle* eagerly published.

This was to be the first appearance of "Der Judenstaat," in condensed form; a month later in 1895, it was published in its entirety in Vienna. "Der Judenstaat," which translated means "The Jewish State," was so stunningly simple and direct, so urgent and clear in its thesis, that it was to unite decisively a great portion of the disparate elements and viewpoints among late nineteenth-century Jewry.

"Judenstaat" was a clarion call to Jews around the world. Perhaps it was the direct, vernacular style of the former journalist, perhaps it was Herzl's call to Jews to help themselves, to choose dignity over submission, but it quickly became something around which the Jewish people could rally: a clear, definitive, thoughtful, how-to guide to Zionist independence. "The idea which I have developed in this pamphlet is a very old one," he wrote. "It is a restoration of the Jewish state."

In Tel Aviv in 1949, with Israeli airmen standing guard, the body of Theodore Herzl, the father of modern Zionism and the first modern advocate of a separate homeland for the Jews, was placed on a special altar in the square in front of the Israeli parliament. His body was brought by air from Vienna, where Herzl died in 1904, and was reinterred in the new Jewish state as per his request at the time of his death.

Herzl's tract, which was subtitled "An Attempt at a Modern Solution of the Jewish Question," had found the right audience at the right time and with the right words: "I shall now put the question in the briefest possible form: Are we to 'get out' and where to? Or may we yet remain? And how long?" Whatever the reason, Herzl succeeded where others had only made dents in persuading the Jews that it was time for them to realize that they *were* a nation, but without a homeland.

Within eighteen months of the publication of "Judenstaat," Herzl organized and convened the first Zionist Congress in Basel, Switzerland. The Congress, which was a stroke of genius, convened biennially thereafter (always in different nations) and was instrumental in galvanizing not only Jewish thought but action too. Indeed, the Congress was to become the chief organ of Jewish statehood until the actual creation of the state of Israel some fifty years later.

The first Congress was convened in 1897, presided over by Herzl, and attended by two hundred delegates from fifteen countries: a clear statement that the Jews were ready to take statehood seriously. Among other milestones, the Congress saw the successful establishment of an official Zionist Colonial Trust as well as the inauguration of an official Zionist press that was to publish books and pamphlets in many languages. In his diary, following his stirring keynote speech at that first Congress, Herzl commented: "Here I have created the Jewish state."

Over the next eight years Herzl would work tirelessly in an effort to reestablish the state of Israel in Palestine. This included pursuing and meeting with the leaders of Turkey, Germany, Prussia, Italy, England, and Russia. He even met with the Pope in an effort to gain his support for the establishment of the Jewish nation (the Pope was not supportive). He also led delegations to Palestine and Constantinople, and in general fought unrelentingly for the Jewish nation that he knew would come to be.

Herzl died of heart complications in 1904 at the age of forty-four. A personally charismatic leader, Herzl's efforts to unite his people, and to rally them around not only the notion of statehood but also the steps necessary to achieve it, were remarkable.

In 1949, when the State of Israel celebrated its first anniversary, Herzl's coffin was transferred to Jerusalem and buried on a hilltop called Mount Herzl.

At the 7th International Jewish Congress, held in Basel in 1905, Chaim Weizmann—who would later become the first president of Israel—emerged as a leader. Weizmann believed that Herzl's efforts to gain international financial support for the outright purchase of lands in Palestine for the State of Israel had failed. He advocated using all funds available to the movement for a more practical, gradual resettlement of Palestine by pioneers. Though it took some time, Weizmann's view eventually won the support of the Congress in 1911. It was this subtler approach—colonization of the Promised Land by a slow but steady stream of Jewish settlers—that would prove most effective in bringing about the restoration of Israel as the Jewish state.

Dr. Chaim Weizmann (1847-1952) became the first president of Israel in 1949. His efforts as leader of the Zionist movement between World War I and World War II were instrumental in effecting the formation of the Jewish state. Of particular importance was his influence with Arthur Balfour, whose legendary Balfour Declaration was hailed as a turning point in Jewish and Zionist history.

The Balfour Declaration

The relationship between Britain and the Jewish people that began in the eighteenth century and was solidified in the nineteenth century was as instrumental to the formation of the State of Israel as Herzl's call to statehood and Weizmann's practical settlement of Palestine. In Britain, Jews had complete freedom of citizenship and an open-door policy with respect to immigration from 1826 onward.

Britain was not just hospitable to Jewish immigrants, it was also prepared to help Jews abroad with moral support and practical aid whenever anti-Semitic surges resulted in their expulsion or persecution. Thus it was that the British came to the aid of the Jewish people a number of times during the nineteenth century: in 1854, on behalf of the Swiss Jews; in 1856, in the Balkans; and at the Congress of Berlin in 1876, at which Disraeli spoke and fought for equality of religious rights.

In fact, British efforts during the period 1827–1839 were largely responsible for the rise in the Jewish population of Jerusalem from 550 to 5,000, and in Palestine as a whole to as many as 10,000 Jews. In 1838, Lord Palmerston, a member of Parliament who personally was dedicated to the idea of returning Jews to Jerusalem, made appointments and disseminated a diplomatic agenda among the Turks and Europeans that encouraged protection of the Jews in the promised land, as well as their return to the homeland from Europe and Asia.

There are certainly many reasons for the strength of the alliance between Jews and the British during this period. Queen Victoria was extremely close to Sir Moses Montefiore (1784–1855), who was a brother-in-law of the powerful Rothschild family. Montefiore, who lived to be one hundred years old, devoted his life to Jewish philanthropy, especially in the realm of fighting anti-

Benjamin Disraeli (1804-1881) was a British statesman and author whose Italian-Jewish roots made him a unique figure in the history of British rule. As prime minister, he was responsible for arranging Great Britain's acquisition of the Suez Canal, thereby putting the nation directly in the path of Jewish history.

Semitism (he was personally responsible, for example, for saving the Jewish community of Damascus during the terror of 1839–1840).

It was perhaps the belief that the Second Coming of Christ would be connected to the return of the Jews to Jerusalem that led the eloquent and audacious Benjamin Disraeli to visit the Holy Land of his ancestors in 1830–1831, even though he was raised a Christian. This visit in turn ignited a lifelong commitment to and belief in the Jews. Both in his novels and in the public policies he advocated, Disraeli maintained a conviction that the Jews were not just equal to other races, but superior. Calling himself "the missing page between the Old Testament and the New," a reference to his Jewish origins and his Christian upbringing, Disraeli worked tirelessly throughout his career to bridge that gap.

Disraeli's greatest claim to fame, aside from being the first (and only) prime minister of England to have been born into the Jewish faith, was England's purchase in 1876 of the Suez Canal. The canal was to be strategically crucial to the predominance of British authority and power in the Middle East. That one act, nearly Disraeli's first and certainly his most stupendous upon becoming prime minister of Britain, was to draw Britain into the politics of the region and set in motion a chain of events and circumstances instrumental to the creation of the State of Israel.

Between 1879 and 1889, Britain proceeded to acquire more than 1.25 million square miles of lands surrounding India, which had come under its domain following the Mutiny of India in 1858. The British Empire expanded into Afghanistan, Burma, Egypt (to protect its purchase of the Suez Canal), and northern Africa. During this period the Palestine Exploration Fund, manned by British soldiers and Royal Engineers, was dispatched to the Middle East—ostensibly to conduct biblical research—though clearly there were tactical reasons why the Empire needed extensive, accurate, and reliable maps of the strategic region's topography and natural resources.

Perhaps the British support of a Jewish presence in Palestine was merely political—Russia to the north was known to periodically attempt a conquest of the Turkish Empire which controlled the region. In 1830, when Tsar Nicholas I attempted to grab the Black Sea, it was Britain that fought back and won; in the 1850s Britain and France united with Turkey against Russia in the Crimean War over the same territorial issue. In 1844, while visiting England, Nicholas I proposed a joint partitioning of the Turkish Empire, with Russia taking possession of the Balkans and Britain gaining sovereignty over Egypt and Crete.

Though the Tsar's proposal was not to come to fruition, in the 1870s the issue was raised again between the two nations and the Russians finally managed to win significant amounts of Turkish-held territory in Europe. But this time the British chose not to fight the Russians; instead, Prime Minister Disraeli secured the strategic island of Cypress for the crown, thereby setting the stage for a future of British rule in Palestine and Syria. Indeed by 1878, when the Cypress Convention gave Britain the island of Cypress in exchange for its vow to protect the Sultan of Turkey's territories in Asia (including the Middle East), the British were prepared to keep Palestine (among other territories) from the Russians at any cost. By the time Disraeli died in 1880, Palestine was well on its way to coming within the sphere of the British Empire.

By 1885, however, Lord Salisbury, heading the Foreign Office for the British Empire, began to come to the conclusion that the British had taken the wrong side in signing the Cypress Convention and placing itself in opposition to Russia. Moreover, it was quite apparent that the Turks were increasingly alienated from the British, who at any rate had never really felt any confidence in the Turks, only an abiding opposition to Russian rule in the Middle East. So as Lord Salisbury concentrated his diplomatic and imperial efforts upon Egypt, the Sultan, in Constantinople, turned his hopes to the rising power of Germany.

Neville Chamberlain (1869-1940), British Colonial Office chief, was supportive of the idea of a Jewish land, and suggested several sites, including one in Uganda. Ironically, later, as prime minister, Chamberlain's policies of appeasement with respect to Adolf Hitler failed to avert the outbreak of World War II, a failure that was to have catastrophic results in terms of the history of the Jews.

Indeed, the Cypress Convention wasn't satisfactory to the Sultan of Turkey either. It had left him mistrustful of the British crown and its representatives, since it in effect gave them the right to invade his country. By the early decades of the twentieth century this rift between Britain and the Turks would lead Turkey, increasingly, to Germany. Perhaps Germany, which in the nineteenth century was neither expansionist nor patriarchal, seemed less threatening to the self-interests of the Sultan.

Even as the Turks were losing control of increasingly larger chunks of the Middle East, the efforts of the Lovers of Zion had resulted in a small but effective Jewish presence in Jaffa: by 1889, 76,000 acres of land spread over twenty-two settlements were inhabited by 5,000 Jewish pioneers. Poorly prepared for the desert conditions of the region, the Lovers of Zion were barely surviving, and might have failed totally were it not for a trickle (and later a stream) of funding that arrived via the Rothschild family.

It was around this time that the British Colonial Office chief, Lord Neville Chamberlain (whose nephew Albert Balfour was then Prime Minister of England), made himself available to Theodor Herzl for discussion of possible sites for the location of a Jewish state, although the word statehood was never explicitly stated. Herzl suggested Cypress, El Arish, and the Sinai Peninsula as suitable regions for resettlement. Chamberlain suggested a region in East Africa—somewhere near Uganda—as a possible site for the Jewish nation. Although the talks between Chamberlain and Herzl eventually fell apart, the significance of a representative of a major European Empire actually discussing the possibility of land assignments with a mere leader of a political movement was a matter of historic importance.

Arthur James Balfour (1848-1930), an English states-man who served as prime minister and then foreign secretary to Prime Minister Lloyd George starting in 1916, became an ardent Zionist following two brief but momentous encounters with Chaim Weizmann. He was the author of the Balfour Declaration of 1917, which pledged support for a Jewish National Home in Palestine. His declaration was the product of his idealism, his admiration for Weizmann, and his belief that centuries of crimes against the Jews required an act of restoration "to wash out an ancient stain upon our own civilization."

However, the Zionist Congress rejected Chamberlain's offer of an African settlement. Here at last was the reemergence of the Jewish identification with the land known as Palestine—with the land itself. Thus, Zionism was not merely a quest for statehood, then, but a mission for a particular piece of land: to restore Eretz Yisrael, hallowed ground, to the Jewish people.

The rejection of the African land got the attention of Balfour. Curious as to the reasons behind the Zionists' strong reaction to the offer, Balfour met with Weizmann in 1906. Though the meeting was undertaken somewhat casually and, as said, mainly out of curiosity, it was to prove crucial both in terms of the relationship that was to arise between Balfour and Weizmann and in terms of the ultimate fate of Palestine and the Jews.

Balfour, as it turned out, had had a lifelong fascination both with the Old Testament and with the Jews. By all accounts, Balfour's interest in the Jews had a kind of purity: he simply believed that the right thing to do was to return Palestine to the Jews.

Christianity, he believed, owed the exiles a huge debt.

When the two men met in 1906, Weizmann sought to make it clear to Balfour why it was that the Jews had to have Jerusalem back, why no substitute could possibly replace this goal of Jewish nationhood. Palestine, Weizmann told Balfour, was a matter of faith where the Jews were concerned. It was a passionate and, as it would turn out, historic meeting; Balfour was to consider it one of the most memorable of his life.

Though Balfour and Weizmann were not to meet again until 1914, their second meeting would result in a lifelong friendship, and would further convince Balfour of the justness of the restoration of the holy land to the Jews. It is said that, upon their second meeting, Weizmann moved Balfour to tears with his eloquent explication of the plight of the stateless Jew in Europe (never a Jew and never a European either).

When World War I erupted in the summer of 1914, the Turks elected to align themselves with Germany. This would prove to be a decisive moment in the history of the Turkish rule of Palestine, and therefore in the history of the Jews, for the British and its allies were completely victorious, and the former domains of the Ottoman Empire fell to them to divide and conquer: Palestine, Mesopotamia, Arabia, Turkey, the Sinai desert, El Arish, Gaza, Jaffa, Jerusalem, and finally, all of Syria.

In November 1917, the British passed into legislation the Balfour Declaration, thanks to Balfour himself, now serving as Foreign Secretary to Zionist and Prime Minister Lloyd George. It had been significantly modified from its original intent, to establish Palestine as the Jewish homeland, and gave the Jews the right to emigrate and settle there and the right to the creation of an internally autonomous government.

The crucial paragraph of the Declaration read: "His Majesty's Government view with favor the establishment in Palestine of a national home for the Jewish people, and will use their best efforts to facilitate the achievement of this object, it being clearly understood that nothing shall be done which may prejudice the civil and religious rights of existing non-Jewish communities in Palestine, or the rights and political status enjoyed by Jews in any other country."

David Lloyd George (1863-1945) was Prime Minister of England from 1916 to 1922, and is therefore credited as the leader of the government that was to pass the Balfour Declaration. Lloyd George, like his secretary Balfour, was a lifelong Zionist. In 1903, Lloyd George acted as legal advisor to Theodore Herzl in connection with an aborted plan to settle the Jewish people in East Africa.

Regardless of the individual players in the events leading up to the declaration, Britain had to do something with the Middle East. The period following the end of the war was nightmarish, a carnival of claims and disputes over the Holy Land made by Jews, Arabs, Zionists, and anti-Zionists. And the British had their own political agenda to pursue. The Palestine Campaign undertaken ostensibly to protect the Empire's ownership of the Suez Canal and to protect trade routes to its territories in the East, had put all of the ancient lands of Canaan under British control. The Balfour Declaration somewhat restored the biblical promised land to the Jews—and also tacitly assured the British of a buffer nation that would provide a bridge between the East and Europe.

While the Balfour Declaration emerged in its final form somewhat less decisive in its creation of a Jewish state than Weizmann (and indeed Balfour) might have at first hoped and dreamed, there is no doubt that the Declaration was instrumental in the ultimate establishment of the state of Israel. It was a momentous achievement, too, since under the criteria applied at the

Versailles settlement after the war the Jews had no claim to Palestine left save an historical and romantic notion of a homeland thousands of years old. At the time of the Declaration there were only about 100,000 Jews actually living in Palestine—whereas there were some 500,000 Arabs.

Both kibbutzim and moshavim are unique forms of cooperative living developed in the early part of the twentieth century. Kibbutzim are organized around the concept of a self-contained social and economic unit. By contrast, moshavim are organized around the notion of autonomous families linked socially but not economically.

While the Balfour Declaration was hailed as the restoration of a nation, the realization of the vision of the prophet Isaiah, the return to Palestine of the flowing lands of milk and honey, the redemption of the promise carried in the hearts of the Jewish people since the destruction of the temple in Jerusalem—in short every idealization of the biblical lands of Canaan promised by God to the Jews—it was the Palestinian Mandate that made it a matter of law. Signed and ratified in 1922 by the Principal Allied Powers through the League of Nations, the Mandate gave Britain responsibility for Palestine. It transformed the idealism of Balfour into a tangible, international commitment on the part of the British to oversee the restoration of Israel in Palestine.

Of the Arabs, only Emir Feisal, leader of the Hashemites, was favorably disposed toward the Jews: "We Arabs," he wrote, "especially the educated among us, look with the deepest sympathy upon the Zionist movement. . . . We will wish the Jews a most hearty welcome home." Unfortunately, the welcome was short-lived, and by March 1920 there were Arab riots in Jerusalem and attacks on Jewish settlers in Galilee. The next struggle was just beginning: to eke out a nation in a hostile land, to unite a people scattered by time, inclination, and geography, under an edict whose stipulations would prove difficult to accommodate.

Aliyah

When the British took Palestine from the Turks early in the twentieth century, there were two types of Jews then living in the region: those who had been there since the fall of Jerusalem in 70 C.E. and whose population had grown during the nineteenth century, a deeply religious and scholarly community that resided within the Jewish quarter of the Old City of Jerusalem and was largely dependent upon the charity of international Jewish funds to survive; and the agricultural settlers, who began arriving in Palestine toward the end of the nineteenth century, financed by wealthy Jewish philanthropic groups and families like the Montefiores and the Rothschilds. Most of the latter began arriving in Palestine after the horrific Russian progroms of 1881. This period of Jewish migration to Israel became known as the first Aliyah (which means "ascent").

In the early part of the twentieth century, thousands of Jewish teenagers and young adults fled lands where they were persecuted and came to Palestine seeking a new life and greater opportunities in a movement known as the Youth Aliyah.

Through the philanthropy of Edmund de Rothschild alone, Jewish settlers were provided with administrators, schools, and doctors for their new settlements, villages that were called *moshavot*. Moshavot funded in 1881 by Rothschild included Ekron, Gederah, Rishon le-Zion, and Petah Tikva in Judea; Rosh Pinha and Yesud ha-Ma'ala in Galilee; and Zikhron Yacov in Samaria. In 1896, Metullah and Be'er Toviyyah, founded by Russian Zionists, also benefited from Rothschild's philanthropy.

In 1904, the second and much larger Aliyah began, inspired by even more dreadful violence in Russia: 40,000 new immigrants found their way to Palestine at this time. In 1909, a new garden suburb was founded near Jaffa that was later to become the thriving, cosmopolitan city of Tel Aviv.

Also in 1909, the first kibbutz was founded at Deganya. Kibbutzim, or voluntary collective farms, were the main kind of work settlement sponsored and funded by the Zionists' systematic settlement efforts. Eventually, the Zionists would sponsor some two hundred such farms. This period also saw the development of Moshav Ovedim, agricultural villages where land was privately owned by settlers but equipment was purchased cooperatively. Moshav Shittifi, which also sprang up at this time, were agricultural villages in which residents owned their own homes but worked land that was cooperatively owned by the village.

To defend the settlements, the society of Shomerim, or "Watchmen," was founded in 1909. The Shomerim were mostly groups of young Jewish immigrants from Russia who had learned something about self-defense to resist the pogroms. They appear to have been something of a ragtag organization, until they came under the leadership of Vladimir Jabotinsky. Jabotinsky, who came from Odessa, a city whose Jewish population in the 1900s was 170,000 strong, had distinguished himself as a powerful writer and orator, and his work in the Jewish press established him as a prominent Zionist of the period. He was also a member of the Odessa self-defense force.

When World War I erupted, Jabotinsky was given an assignment to cover the Middle East as a correspondent for a Moscow newspaper. In Palestine he found the Turks persecuting the Jews, whose numbers (as high as 85,000 before the war), had dwindled to 60,000. In Alexandria, 10,000 Jews were barely surviving. Ashkenazim and Sephardim were divided by differences in worship

Vladimir Jabotinsky (1880-1940) was a Zionist leader and founder of the Revisionist movement, which began in 1925 at a conference in Paris. His aims were immediate mass Jewish immigration and settlement in Palestine, the formation of a Jewish militia, the creation of a Jewish majority in Palestine on both sides of the Jordan river, and, finally, Jewish statehood upon achievement of that majority. A political foe of both Weizmann and the policies and goals of the official Zionist movement, Jabotinsky's followers would eventually become a right-wing minority within Palestine and during the early formation of the state of Israel.

rituals. Students attending a new gym in Tel Aviv refused to heed any instructions not delivered to them in Hebrew. When Jabotinsky arrived in Palestine and saw the inner and outer strife under which the Jews there were living, he determined that only an army could bring them together.

Joining forces with Joseph Trumpeldor (1880–1920), Jabotinsky founded the Zion Mule Corps, and later the two men formed three battalions of Royal Fusiliers. This Jewish army participated in the war against the Turks, fighting on the side of the British. When the war ended, however, there was no specific Zionist mandate to keep the Jewish Legion going, and the British promptly disbanded it. So Jabotinsky formed a covert Jewish self-defense organization, which eventually became the Haganah—the seed of what was to become a mighty army.

Jabotinsky likely saw the continued need for a Jewish army given the growing Arab hostility toward the Jewish settlements, which in turn had its source in the Arabs' own developing sense of nationalist spirit. Whereas the Jewish nationalist movement arose out of the European nationalism of the nineteenth century, the Arab sense of nationalism started somewhat later. Al-Fatah, the Young Arabs, founded in Paris in 1911, was inspired by the rise of nationalism among the Afro-Asian peoples in the early twentieth century and in Palestine by the war itself. After the war, France, which had become the seat of some anti-British and anti-Zionist feelings (at least in part a reaction to the mandates of the Balfour Declaration), encouraged Al-Fatah to set up its home base in French-controlled Damascus.

After the war the Arabs were given French protectorates in Syria and Lebanon, and British protectorates in Palestine, Transjordan, and Iraq. Only the Saudis in Arabia, lead by Emir Feisal of the Hashemites, were given sovereignty, in a region of the Transjordan.

At the war's end, Jews were free to migrate once more from Europe and Russia into Egypt and Palestine; indeed, great military and political powers were conspiring to see that they did. Despite the favorable response to the notion of a Jewish presence in

Palestine among more moderate Arabs, unrest fired up by more radical elements lead to Arab attacks on Jewish settlements beginning in March 1920 in Galilee and Jerusalem.

Jabotinksy's Haganah attempted to defend the Jewish settlers, and his soldiers were arrested and given fifteen years' hard labor, as were the Arab rioters who had started everything (both sides were later given amnesty, however). In response to the unrest, the British sent Herbert Samuel, who had participated in the development and passage of the Balfour Declaration and who also happened to be the first Jewish member of Parliament, as high commissioner.

In 1921, Winston Churchill (1874-1965), then colonial secretary to the British Government, and Sir Herbert Samuel (1870 - 1963), then the British High Commissioner of Palestine, visited Jerusalem in an effort to sort out the tense and tangled post-war situation in the Middle East. Among the measures taken to stem Arab rioting in the region in 1920 and 1921 were the exclusion of the Transjordan from the settlement area defined by the Jewish National Home policy.

Samuel, who was an atheist Jew and a non-Zionist committed to the idea of a Jewish homeland, made it his mission to teach the Jews and the Arabs to live together in Palestine—to effect a compromise for the sake of the nation. He was pragmatic, and his efforts to persuade the Zionists of the importance of gaining the cooperation of local, existing non-Jewish communities were worthwhile. Unfortunately, the Zionists had their hands full just sustaining their settlements.

In March 1921, Samuel was to make the mistake (no doubt coming out of his spirit of appeasement) of appointing a radical Arab leader, Haji Ami al-Husaini, to what was regarded as a minor post, Grand Mufti of Jerusalem, thereby setting the stage for the "official" promotion of anti-Zionist, radical Arab politics in Jerusalem. This would open a chasm between Jewish and Arab leaders that would take decades to bridge.

The Mufti promoted pan-Arabism and anti-Zionism, he was ruthless (and killed many Arabs who got in his way), and was eventually to become Britain's most outstanding opponent and Hitler's greatest ally in the Middle East . Until 1947, Husaini and his followers ruled Palestinian political strategy. Their refusal to negotiate directly with the Jews, which would ultimately force them into unilateral action, is considered the primary reason that the Arabs lost Palestine.

For had it not been for these extremists, leaders like Feisal—who had received Weizmann at his desert headquarters in 1918 upon Weizmann's arrival in the Middle East as leader of the Zionist Commission—and Sherif Hussein, the Sherif of Mecca—who published a newspaper article at that same time welcoming the Jews and exhorting the Arabs to greet them as brothers—might have prevailed, and the State of Israel might have simply encompassed the tiny, 10,434 square miles (27,128 sq. km), one percent of

Arab territories liberated by the British in 1918, that had originally been mandated for the Jews by Balfour. Samuel remained high commissioner of Palestine until 1925, when Lord Plumer took over (1925–1928).

The growth of Jewish settlements in Palestine was slow due to Arab resistance and a difference of opinion on policy and methods among the Jewish leadership. Whereas Weizmann had always advocated a gradual, patient resettlement of the promised land, other leaders disagreed.

On May 14, 1948 in a small Tel Aviv art museum, David Ben-Gurion stood before thirty-seven of his colleagues and read out the State of Israel's Proclamation of Independence, establishing the opening of the Israeli parliament. The attendees each signed the proclamation, and promptly appointed a provisional government with Ben-Gurion as prime minister and minister of defense.

In the 1920s, one great political force emerged in Israel from a differing ideological camp: David Ben-Gurion (1886–1973). He was firmly collectivist in his views, and felt that what mattered most was the political and economic stability of Israel. A socialist, Ben-Gurion was born David Green in Poland, where as a young man he was an early leader of Zionist youth groups and workers' organizations. He changed his last name to Ben-Gurion (which means "son of a lion cub") in 1906 when, at the age of twenty, he immigrated to Eretz Yisrael. Following his arrival in Jaffa, he moved around during his twenties, ranging over the lands of the Middle East and even traveling as far afield as New York, where he went in 1915 following his banishment from Palestine by the Turks.

At war's end he returned to Palestine, and by 1920 joined the Haganah and was appointed general-secretary of the newly founded General Federation of Palestine Jewish Workers. During the ensuing decades Ben-Gurion joined, formed, or oversaw the merging of numerous organizations, all with the common goal of the settlement of Israel. He would eventually become the first prime minister of Israel. Often called the George Washington of Israel, Ben-Gurion led his people through the most difficult period of its growth—the early years when the land was least forgiving, the neighbors most hostile, and the nation most tender. Directing settlement of the lands to its furthest reaches, Ben-Gurion safeguarded the nation's future. Until his death in 1973, he worked tirelessly to make Israel a better place to live, for he believed that Jewish redemption depended on the Jews themselves.

Ben-Gurion's politics differed from Weizmann's in the unwavering commitment to a speedy settlement of the promised land, especially by Jews who were willing to work the land and did not shy away from hard labor. His own, personal brand of Zionism was founded on what were to become three basic principles from which he never deviated: that Jews must make it a priority to return to Zion, because settlement of the land itself is "the only true Zionism"; that the new community should be structured along a socialist framework; and that Hebrew must become the official, culturally binding language of the new society.

Thus the direction the Jewish state was to take was affected deeply by a difference of opinion among three or four different political parties. Ben-Gurion advocated the immigration of pioneers who could work the land, primarily a socialist or labor view. Weizmann, whose eye was on the establishment of institutions, represented the British view, which was to settle Palestine slowly. Both men were in favor of increasing the population, and both were hostile to the aims of the religious wing of the Zionists, which founded the Mizrachi Party to encourage the immigration of Jews from the Polish ghettos to the city of Tel Aviv (where they supported the growth of capitalism and land speculation). Jabotinsky espoused a Revisionist view on immigration, simply wanting numbers.

Jabotinsky seceded from the Zionist executive party in 1923 and two years later founded the Union of Zionist-Revisionists, the goal of which was to bring to Palestine "the largest number of Jews within the shortest period of time." This party elicited a huge following in Eastern Europe, where Betar, a revisionist, militant Jewish youth party, was training its members to shoot guns, wear uniforms, and drill. Menachim Begin, who would one day lead Israel to peace with Egypt, was a member of Betar.

By the 1930s, the Jews had three political parties: the World Zionist Congress, from which Weizmann was driven from the presidency in 1931 by the Mizrachi; Ben Gurion's political party, a group of merged interests called, collectively, the Mapai, or Zionist Labor Party; and Jabotinsky's Revisionists. Infighting, especially among the Mapai and the Revisionists, was to cast a shadow over the Zionist state from its very first days.

In 1982, Prime Minister Menachim Begin (1913-1992) addressed the 30th Zionist Congress, telling delegates that Israel would demand that all PLO forces be withdrawn from Lebanon before Israel would consider a pullback of its own forces as well as Syrian troops. Begin was later to meet U.S. envoy Philip Habib for further talks on getting negotiations started with Lebanon.

The decade of the 1920s was a prosperous one throughout Europe, following as it did the turmoil of the war, and most Jews were simply too content with the prosperity to be willing to shuck it all, pull up roots, and sail for Palestine—whether it be Eretz Yisrael or not. That said, however, the Jewish population there did double to 160,000 during the 1920s. The number of agricultural villages, or kibbutzim, also doubled. The establishment of kibbutzim was the main goal of a third Aliyah of settlers— 37,000 of whom arrived from Poland and Lithuania between 1919 and 1923. A fourth Aliyah was composed of roughly 60,000 Ashkenazi Jews from eastern Europe, most of whom settled in Tel Aviv and Haifa.

By 1929, when Jewish security in Europe began to deteriorate along with the prosperity, the tide began to turn. Suddenly hundreds of thousands of Jews were eager to relocate. In 1934, 40,000 Jews emigrated to Palestine. In 1935, that number increased to 62,000 as the full meaning of Hitler's chancellery and concomitant persecution of Germany's Jews sparked a fifth flight to

Concentration camp prisoners gather behind barbed wire, awaiting liberation. Before the start of Hitler's war on the Jews, there were roughly 8,861,800 Jews living in the parts of Europe that would directly or indirectly come under his control. Of that number, it is estimated that the Nazis killed 67 percent, or 5,933,900 Jews.

Palestine. But as the immigrants flooded in, the Arab response grew more violent, and by July 1937 a British commission under Lord Peel recommended that Jewish immigration be reduced to 12,000 individuals per year and that land purchases be restricted as well.

The Peel Commission also broached, for the first time, the possibility of a three-way partition of Palestine: the coastal strip, Galilee, and the Jezreel Valley to be formed into a Jewish state; the hills of Judea, the Negev, and Ephraim into an Arab state; and a mandatory, British-run enclave to be formed from Jerusalem through Lydda and Ramleh to Jaffa. The Arabs rejected the proposal with rage and staged another uprising in 1937. The following year, a pan-Arab conference was held in Cairo, and the first pan-Arab pledge to take international action to prevent further development of a Zionist state was made.

In 1939, in the face of the extreme hostility of the Arab response to the Tripartite Conference in London, the British dropped the proposal, and allowed the Balfour Declaration to be quietly buried. Instead, the British advocated in a "white paper" (a government report) that only 75,000 more Jews be permitted to move to Palestine over the course of five years, and thereafter none at all. Though there were now 500,000 Jews living in Palestine, the Arabs still constituted a vast majority. The new British politics of appeasement would soon have drastic consequences for the Jews.

The Holocaust carried out by Nazi Germany and its allies against Europe's 8,861,800 Jews in the late 1930s and early 1940s was horrific. There has never been a more total, systematic destruction of the Jews. Unlike the expulsions and exiles of the fifteenth century, the German attack upon the Jews was designed to strip them, little by little, of every shred of human decency—to isolate, overwork, demean, ostracize, impoverish, and defeat them—prior to annihilating them. Even worse than the ideological crusades of the first century that led to the destruction of Jerusalem and the dispersion of the Jewish people, the Nazi campaign of hatred that resulted in what was to become known as the "Final Solution" (which began in 1939) is the most evil event in modern or ancient history. It is difficult to grasp how Germany, a nation that had heroically saved the Jewish people from the bloody pogroms of

the Russian Empire just fifty years earlier, could become so unthinkably bloody and so filled with hate.

While even this tragedy did not succeed in eradicating world anti-Semitism (it merely displaced its center from Europe to

the Middle East), the Holocaust did create an international mandate for both

punishment and reparations. Thus, whereas World War I made a Zionist state

possible, World War II made it essential. Not only because it created an interna-

tional debt to the Jews, but also because it united the overwhelming majority of

them in a single purpose: the imperative that a Jewish nation had to be created

and made secure no matter what.

Eretz Yisrael

During the war, Jewish immigration to Palestine remained limited by the white

paper of 1939. But the Jews were Britain's ally during the war and so, as Ben-

Gurion put it best, it was up to them to "fight Hitler as though there were no

White Paper, and fight the White Paper as though there were no Hitler."

After the Alamein episode of 1942 eliminated the German threat to the

Middle East, Weizmann proposed that the British cooperate with small-scale Jewish units

to form a strike force. Winston Churchill, by now Prime Minister of Britain, liked the idea

of the Jews fighting back against the Germans, and the Jewish Brigade, numbering 25,000

soldiers, was formed soon after. Yet despite the assistance of the Jews in the war effort,

the British continued to enforce their immigration policies in the Middle East, even going

so far as to hunt down and deport illegal Jewish immigrants.

In 1947 in Haifa, 4,700 homeless Jews from Europe aboard the S.S. Exodus were turned away by the British, who refused to let them remain in Palestine. Their hopes of starting a new life in the promised land still strong, some of the illegal immigrants attempted to leave the battle-damaged Exodus, resulting in a collision with a British ship. Here, passengers of the tragic voyage are shown standing by the ship's wreckage.

Menachim Begin, most of whose family in Poland had been murdered by the Germans, survived interrogations by Stalin's

NKVD in Lithuania and a Soviet slave-camp in the Arctic Circle long enough to be freed under a Polish amnesty, whereupon he

walked across Central Asia and made his way to Jerusalem as a private in the Polish army. By December 1943 he had taken control

of the Revisionist party's military arm, called Irgun, which two months later declared war on the British, prevailing upon the Jews of

Palestine to revolt and set up a provisional government.

There were three different schools of thought on the issue of the British: the Haganah, including Weizmann and Ben-Gurion (who was focused on winning the war first and dealing with the British later), continued to advocate dealing with the British on a good-faith basis; a radical offshoot of the Revisionists under the leadership of Yitzhak Shamir, among others, carried

In 1948, Israeli Prime Minister David Ben-Gurion, with his wife, friends, and an honor guard bearing the national flag of Israel, came to the docks of Haifa to watch the last contingent of British troops leave the Holy Land. The troops' departure marked the first time since Allenby's campaign in 1917 that the land of Israel was unoccupied by a single British soldier.

out an unrestricted campaign against the British; and Begin's Irgun targeted the British administration in Palestine, not Britain itself.

Though at first Begin's policy was disdained by the Haganah, by October 1945 Ben-Gurion was ready to send a secret message to the commander of the Haganah forces (without Weizmann's knowledge) instructing them to begin operations against the British. The Jewish Resistance Movement was formed thereafter.

Despite the resistance, the British continued its policy of turning away Jewish refugees. In retaliation, the Haganah blew up nine strategic bridges in Palestine. This resulted in a British raid on Jewish headquarters which, though it produced the arrests of some 3,000 Jews—including most of the key Zionist leaders—only served to strengthen Begin and the Irgun. On July 22, 1946, the Irgun bombed the King David Hotel, the British headquarters, and though the British had been amply warned of the impending attack, they were nonetheless shocked when an entire wing of the hotel exploded and collapsed.

The British proposed, again, a tripartite division of the country. This time it was rejected by both Jews and Arabs. Finally, on February 14, 1947, Foreign Secretary Ernest Bevin threw up his hands and turned the entire matter of Palestine over to the United Nations.

Once the British renounced their mandate, U.S. President Harry S. Truman pushed for the creation of a Jewish state in Palestine. When the matter came before the assembly two plans were floated and one, with Truman's backing, was ratified. On November 29, 1947, the General Assembly voted 33 to 13 (with ten abstentions) to enact a partition plan that would create a Jewish and an Arab state, as well as an international zone in Jerusalem.

Although in years to come the Soviets would decry the State of Israel as the creation of the imperialist-capitalist war machine (or some such), it is in fact the case that in 1947 Soviet Deputy Foreign Minister Andrei Gromyko surprised the world when he announced that his government was in favor of the plan that eventually passed. Indeed, the entire Soviet bloc voted in favor of the Israeli interest. On May 14, 1948, Israel declared its independence. President Truman immediately gave the nation de facto recognition. Stalin, not to be outdone, gave the nation recognition de jure.

The Arab response to the creation of the state of Israel was armed resistance. When the first partition had been proposed in 1937 the Arabs would have been given 80 percent of Palestine; with the U.N. partition they were given 50 percent. During the war that followed Israel's declaration of independence, from June to November 1948, the Arabs lost control of another 30 percent of Palestine. In 1949, still willing to negotiate with the Arabs, the Israelis attempted to settle with its neighbors upon permanent frontiers—and was prepared to give up some of the territory it had won in the battles of 1948. But the Arabs would not even talk to the Israelis. Indeed, it was not until Menachim Begin, as president of Israel in 1978, and Anwar Sadat, the president of Egypt, negotiated and signed a peace treaty in 1979 with the help of U.S. President Jimmy Carter, that any Arab state was to recognize and make peace with Israel.

In 1956, in Cairo, with tension mounting over Egyptian President Gamal Abdul Nasser's (1918-1970) seizure of the Suez Canal and British Prime Minister Sir Anthony Eden's (1897-1977) description of the crisis as a "battle of life or death for us," preparations in the event of an open conflict over the dispute were made on both sides. In Egypt, modern tank troops (shown above standing for inspection) as well as the old camel corps were alerted.

For the first thirty years of its existence Israel was faced with constant opposition from its Arab neighbors, exacerbated by the battle for world dominance between the Soviet Union (who began providing arms to the Arabs) and the United States (who funded Israel).

In the 1950s Egypt kept the Israelis from access to both the Suez Canal and the Gulf of Aqaba, forcing a brief war for access that left Israel, the victor, with possession of the Sinai peninsula, including Gaza. When the Sinai War ended, Israel agreed to withdraw from the peninsula provided that Egypt did not remilitarize the area. With the aid of U.N. peacekeeping forces, this truce lasted for ten years.

In 1967, however, Egyptian president Gamal Abdel Nasser remilitarized the area and, in cooperation with Jordan and Syria, attempted again to cut Israel off from the canal and the sea. The resulting Six Day War left the victorious Israel in possession of the Left Bank, the Golan Heights in Syria, the Sinai peninsula, and, for the first time in 2,000 years, its former capital: Jerusalem.

In 1973, Egypt, led now by Anwar Sadat (who succeeded Nasser after the latter died), achieved its first victory over Israel with the first battle of the Yom Kippur War. But Israel, though surprised by the attack, held on and won the war. In 1977, Begin's Likud party (a descendent of the Revisionists) took control for the first time in the history of the state, which had been run since its birth by Ben-Gurion's Labor Party. Sadat recognized an opportunity for peace and wasted no time in making an offer. Begin, equally astute, wasted no time in accepting the possibility of trading land for peace. Thus in 1977 and 1978 a momentous peace treaty was negotiated and signed by Israel and Egypt.

In an historic photograph seen round the world, Israeli Prime Minister Yitzhak Rabin and Palestinian leader Yasir Arafat shake hands while United States President Bill Clinton looks on in 1993, at the signing of the peace accord between Israel and the Palestinians. While this handshake was to have ushered in a new era of cooperation, the conflict continues, albeit slightly less virulently.

Because the compromise reached between Egypt and Israel was genuine, it would prove capable of providing a lasting peace. In exchange for Egypt's recognition of Israel's right to exist (as well as iron-clad guarantees of protection along Israel's southern border), Israel handed over the Sinai and much of the West Bank. An attempt was made at this time to negotiate peace with the Palestinians as well—now scattered throughout Israel, Egypt, and, largely, Jordan—but they remained steadfast in their unwillingness to negotiate with the Jews.

The peace treaty between Israel and Egypt, though it cost Begin important political friends, was a major breakthrough in the history of Eretz Yisrael that was not to be matched again until 1993, when the dovish Yitzhak Rabin, in cooperation with Palestinian leader Yassir Arafat, at last forged a peace treaty with the Palestinians, whose Intifada had taken a terrible toll since the late 1980s not only on peace in the Middle East but internationally as well.

Though in 1995 Rabin was assassinated by a young Jew inflamed by the decades of fighting and passions that have defined Israel's first fifty years of nationhood, there is hope worldwide that a lasting peace among all the residents of the Middle East will someday come into existence. In May 1996 Likud party leader Benjamin Netanyahu (1949–) was elected Prime Minister of Israel, the youngest prime minister in Israeli history, and it is now up to him to lead the nation into a twenty-first century of peace with its neighbors. Meanwhile, the breakdown of the Soviet Union, which for decades fueled the fighting among Arabs and Jews, has been a considerable contributing factor to peace efforts in the Middle East.

Despite recurrent war and conflict, Israel has only to continued to grow and prosper. During its first fifty years, the population of the tiny nation has exploded, thanks in part to the Law of Return, passed in 1950, which granted instant citizenship to any

Jew who wished to return to the promised land. In Israel's first three years of existence, 685,000 Jews immigrated there, almost half of them refugees from Europe, doubling the Jewish population. In 1955–1957 there was another huge wave of 160,000 immigrants; in 1961–1964, 215,000 more Jews moved to Israel; and in 1967 the Six Day War stimulated immigration yet again.

By the mid-1980s, the total population of Israel was 3.5 million; worldwide the number of Jews was 13.5 million (a far cry from the population of eighteen million at the end of the 1930s). When the Soviet Union collapsed in 1990, Soviet Jews were allowed to emigrate freely for the first time since the nineteenth century; almost 500,000 Soviet Jews emigrated to the state of Israel between 1990 and 1992, reaffirming once more the crucial place that Israel holds in the world as the only country where Jews will always be welcome, by law.

With all of these immigrants flowing freely into the country, Israel's internal mandate was to provide housing, education, and employment for its new citizens. This was accomplished via a socialist-capitalist system of agriculture and commerce that at once provided for the needs of its citizens and exacted their fair share of work in return. This exchange rarely proved to be a problem, since so many of its new citizens were often escaping intolerable political or social conditions and were only too glad to take part in the dream of freedom that is Israel.

Unable to practice their religion freely in the Soviet Union since the advent of Communism, Russian Jews seized the opportunity to emigrate to Israel that presented itself when the Soviet Union collapsed. Each of the more than half a million Ethiopian and Russian Jews who emigrated to Israel in the early 1990s represents an individual in need of a home.

Economically, too, Israel has been an oasis in the desert, turning what should be dry and dead into verdant, overflowing farmland. In the 1950s, the Israelis began with nothing but potash, bromine, and other minerals mined from the Dead Sea; they created an economy that every month exports $1 billion worth of goods (including the world famous Jaffa oranges) to overseas nations. The land of milk and honey was made to flow once more; where trees were planted, forests now thrive.

The Israeli kibbutzim were pioneers not only of socialist, collective farming but also of drip irrigation, and in the 1960s they were the first to use computerized methods to operate their irrigation systems. Many of these innovations were not the sole work of the kibbutzim, however; for they worked together with Israeli scientists and were often funded by Israeli industrialists. This unity of effort can also be credited with the resounding success of the Israeli army, which was one of the two most important instruments in the development of the nation's strength and prosperity. Thanks to the Israeli Defense Force and its repeated victories against hostile neighbors, the image of the Jew was transformed internationally from a passive victim to a wise and formidable fighter.

But it was the establishment of Hebrew as the official language of the State of Israel that was the most impressive early

achievement of the tiny nation. For until late in the nineteenth century Hebrew was practically a dead language; as a written language and a language of prayer, Hebrew had always remained the primary language of Judaism. But it had fallen from use in the vernacular, spoken by no one as a first or even a second language, especially not the Jews who had lived for centuries in the diaspora. The language of the Bible, however, had always dealt with the daily rituals, the details and practical matters of the home and living. Hebrew was in short a language of

Israeli schoolchildren live and learn in Hebrew, a language once considered dead but revived in the late nineteenth century. The new immigrants wanted to leave behind everything that reminded them of their lives in exile, including their diverse languages. The revival of Hebrew helped bind them as a nation.

conduct and not just a language of prayer, so the words were there waiting for the Jews to speak once more. It was an act of will and faith that caused the Jews of Palestine, starting with the first Aliyah of 1881, to resurrect the language; it was only a matter of time before more and more Jews began to adopt it as their first language.

In 1919, the British recognized Hebrew and gave it equal status with Arabic and English, permitting it to become the official language of the government and of the army. Newly arriving immigrants, including Ben-Gurion (whose name had been Green), adopted Hebrew names in recognition of their newly rediscovered sense of nationhood. In an act of empowerment, the Jews changed their names from the nineteenth-century Austro-Hungarian Empire's mandated list of Germanic names. When Goldie Myerson became Israel's Foreign Minister in 1959, she changed her name to Golda Meir (who would later become Prime Minister of Israel from 1969 to 1974) in accordance with what by then was accepted Israeli Foreign Office practice. But the changing of names aside, the resurrection of the Hebrew language gave Israel an edge that many young nations often lack: a single native tongue.

The nation adopted a parliamentary form of government, using a British model rather than an American model, even though Weizmann, the nation's first president, lobbied aggressively for American-style presidential power. This created a multiparty system that accommodated the many different political voices and factions among the Jews. It was as much modeled on the delegations of the decades-old Zionist Congress, in some ways, as it was on British parliamentary process.

The Triumph of the Spirit

From the thriving metropolis of Tel Aviv to the ancient beauty of the Old City of Jerusalem, from the lush Galilee basin to the fertile coastal plain, from the modern city of Haifa high atop Mount Carmel to the hills of Samaria in the north and Judea in the south, Israel is a testament to the power of its people: be they Sabras, Ashkenazim, Sephardis, Europeans, Americans, or Ethiopians.

Israeli children in 1948 shriek their joy and excitement about the state's independence as they try to get flags to wave. While they may be temporarily unaware of their part in the existence of the State of Israel, they are the future of the new state.

For they are all Jews. For their thousands of years of suffering and persecution, they have been rewarded, at last, with the long-awaited prosperity in the desert that was promised to them by the covenant. The ancient Jews, the Hebrews of the kingdom of Israel, have survived, have returned, and have thrived once more. That is what they were created to do. That is the triumph of the spirit of Eretz Yisrael.

"Be strong and of good courage," exhorts the Book of Joshua to its wandering people, "be not afraid, neither be thou dismayed: for the Lord thy God is with thee withersoever thou goeth."

Part Two

The Land and the People

LEFT AND ABOVE: *Orthodox Jewish men approach and pray at the Western Wall in the Old City of Jerusalem. Kotel HaMa'aravi, as the wall is called in Hebrew, stands more than 50 feet (15m) tall and is constructed primarily of massive carved stone blocks from the Herodian era. Above these blocks is masonry added during the Mameluke and Turkish periods. Though it is popularly believed that this wall was actually part of the remains of the second Temple, it is in fact the retaining wall for the Temple Mount above. Since it is the only remaining piece of the entire Temple complex, however, it has been the focus of Jewish reverence for almost 2,000 years. The Western Wall became known colloquially as the Wailing Wall because for centuries Jews have gathered here to lament the loss of their great temple.*

The Tallis Steps in the Old City of Jerusalem, so-named because of the way the steps' pattern resembles a tallis—a prayer shawl worn by Jewish men—lead from the Jewish Quarter into the Plaza of the Western Wall.

RIGHT: *The Old City of Jerusalem is tiny in comparison to the modern city as a whole, but it houses the majority of the sacred monuments. Though not nearly as large or as cosmopolitan as nearby Tel Aviv, modern Jerusalem boasts more than 500,000 residents. Since 1967, when the eastern and western parts of the city were unified under Israeli rule following the Six Day War, there has been an explosion of new development as well as continued conservation of the Old City's landmarks.*

LEFT: *The narrow streets and alleys of the Old City of Jerusalem are animated today with the lives of the people who continue to live there. Within these byways that surround the Western Wall on three sides are the Armenian Quarter, the Moslem Quarter, the Christian Quarter, and the Jewish Quarter. Throughout the labyrinth of streets and houses are markets, with sellers offering animal skins, peddlers purveying fruit, and hawkers offering souvenirs and trinkets to the many tourists who pass through here daily.*

RIGHT: *Another view into the byzantine alleys of the Old City of Jerusalem. The architecture is marked by tunnels, walkways, wrought iron gates and handrails, and the ubiquitous carved yellow stone that gives the city its golden glow.*

ABOVE: *An overview of the Old City of Jerusalem shows off the exquisite stonework and uniformity of architecture for which the Golden City has become famous.*

LEFT: *The Armenian Convent of St. Jacques, located in the Old City of Jerusalem, boasts a delicate wrought-iron interior gate and vaulted arches. From the beginning of the fourth century C.E., Jerusalem and other locations in Palestine associated with the life of Jesus Christ were Christianized, and convents, churches, and monasteries were established in the region.*

With the skyline of the city of Jerusalem in the background, a father and son study the ancient tablets marking the remains of the dead in the cemetery on the Mount of Olives. This very extensive Jewish cemetery, the oldest of any religion still in use today, houses the remains of Jews patiently awaiting the arrival of the Messiah and the resurrection to follow.

An Orthodox Jew and an Arab pass one another on a street in Jerusalem, underscoring the diversity of the city and the nation. From its widely varied landscape to its Eastern and Western cultures and traditions, Israel is a land of dichotomies, of old and new, of immigrant and native, of constantly changing and blending ideologies and lifestyles.

A Moslem woman standing by the columns of an ancient temple is a testament to the centuries-long presence of Islam in Jerusalem. The Moslem impact upon Jerusalem came in three stages: the first, shortly after the death of Mohammed, came when his followers began to spread the Islamic faith out of Arabia and conquered Jerusalem from the Byzantine Empire in 638 C.E. It was during this period that Caliph Omar built a mosque on the Temple Mount that was later expanded into the Dome of the Rock. The second stage was in 1187 C.E., when the Europeans were defeated by Saladin and the Moslems began a reconstruction of the city. The third period was during the sixteenth century, when Suleiman I built the city ramparts that still stand.

A group of Moslems prays in a mosque in Kfar Quasem, Israel, wearing traditional kaffiyeh head-dresses and black headbands. When Israel was established in 1948, many of the Arabs native to the region were urged to leave by neighboring countries, in protest against the Jewish state. But more than 150,000 stayed on. The result today is an Arab population of almost one million, of which 77 percent are practicing Moslems.

Members of the Eastern Orthodox Church celebrating a church festival is a reminder of the religious freedom that the state of Israel has delivered to its residents. Each religious community is free, both by law and by practice, to exercise its faith, to observe its holidays and weekly days of rest, and to administer its internal affairs.

Christian pilgrims to the Yardenit River near the Sea of Galilee seek to reaffirm their faith through the wearing of white robes, immersion in the river, prayer, hymns, and expressions of joy. It is believed that the baptism of Jesus by John the Baptist took place here near the southern reaches of the Jordan River, not far from Jericho.

The Ethiopian Monastery, also known as Deir es-Sultan, is located in the Old City of Jerusalem, within the Christian Quarter, not far from the Via Dolorosa. The robed Ethiopian monks, generally tall and slender, gentle and shy, live esthetic lives within tiny cells located on the roof of the monastery. Their church is adorned with modern paintings depicting the visit of the Queen of Sheba to King Solomon. It is the Ethopian Christians' belief that this meeting resulted in an intimate union that in turn produced an heir to the Ethiopian royal house.

An Orthodox Jew blows the shofar, or ram's horn, to mark the start of the Jewish New Year, which begins the yearly cycle of Jewish holidays. Many Jewish holidays mark agricultural events, while others commemorate events in Jewish history, and others are biblically ordained.

An Orthodox Jewish man carries roofing material for the hut he will build with his family to observe the holiday of Sukkot, also known as the Feast of the Tabernacles, a harvest festival. Observant Jews celebrating Sukkot traditionally build thatch-roofed huts and decorate them with fruits of the autumn harvest.

ABOVE: Young boys take a break from their daily prayers at the Western Wall. These boys study at a yeshiva, an orthodox Jewish school, where they learn the finer points of Jewish law.

LEFT: A father and son celebrate Sukkot. The boy is holding a lulav, a combination of palm, myrtle, and willow leaves, while his father holds an etrog, a lemon-like fruit. The lulav and etrog are symbols of the holiday.

Children and adults dress up in costumes to celebrate the holiday of Purim, which marks the Jews' escape from a planned massacre in ancient Persia due to the bravery of a Jewish woman, Queen Esther, and her uncle, Mordechai. Street festivals take place in many towns, and a parade is held in Tel Aviv.

75

Women pack matzoh at a bakery, preparing for the Passover holiday. Passover is traditionally preceded by vigorous housecleaning to remove all traces of leavened bread. During the seven-day holiday, no bread is sold in Jewish stores, and even at most hotels matzoh is served instead of bread. This holiday is observed to remember the hardships experienced by the Jews during the time of the Exodus from Egypt, when they were forced to leave so quickly there was no time to make leavened bread.

A Bukharan Bar Mitzvah at the Wailing Wall in Jerusalem is cause for great celebration. These formerly persecuted Russian Jews embrace the freedom of religion in Israel that permits them to practice their traditions. Of the more than 5 million people who live in Israel, 67 percent are Jews (more than half of them native-born), and almost 20 percent are Arabs (mostly Moslem); the remainder are mostly Christian, and there are also Druze, Circassion, and other smaller religious communities. In 1948, the Declaration of the Establishment of the State of Israel guaranteed freedom of religion to the entire population of the tiny nation.

Bukharan bar mitzvahs at the Waiting Wall are not at all uncommon sights in Jerusalem. Not far from the central plaza, in fact, there is a Bukharan Quarter that dates back to the 1890s. There to this day live the descendants of this Central Asian Jewish community. At one time quite wealthy, the group's fortunes fell into decline following the Soviet annexation of their original homeland.

ABOVE: An Ethiopian Jew prays in the Old City of Jerusalem.

LEFT: Many immigrants to Israel find assimilation to their new homeland difficult, particularly for Ethiopian Jews for whom moving to Israel involves learning not only a new language, but a whole new way of life.

Before arriving in Israel, most of the more than 40,000 Ethiopian Jews who now live there had been illiterate subsistence farmers living in simple villages. Living in their new country means getting used to a far more technologically advanced society than the one they left behind, though there is still time for socializing with friends and family.

A pedestrian walking through the streets of Tel Aviv, where roughly one-third of the nation's population—1.3 million Israelis—occupy about fifty-five square miles (143 sq. km). Tel Aviv was nothing but empty sand dunes when Jewish settlers began arriving here in the 1880s. At first a collection of separate neighborhoods, the city gradually grew together, becoming an oftentimes eccentric mix of Mediterranean-style buildings and skyscrapers. In the 1930s and 1940s, many buildings designed in the International Style by followers of the architects Mies van der Rohe and Le Corbusier began to dominate the scenery.

The ancient-looking limestone of an apartment building contrasts with the sleek modern glass facade of an office building in Tel Aviv, a city that exemplifies Israel's speedy economic growth. While office towers rise in the business district, apartment houses and single-family homes go up in the residential areas, and the population swells.

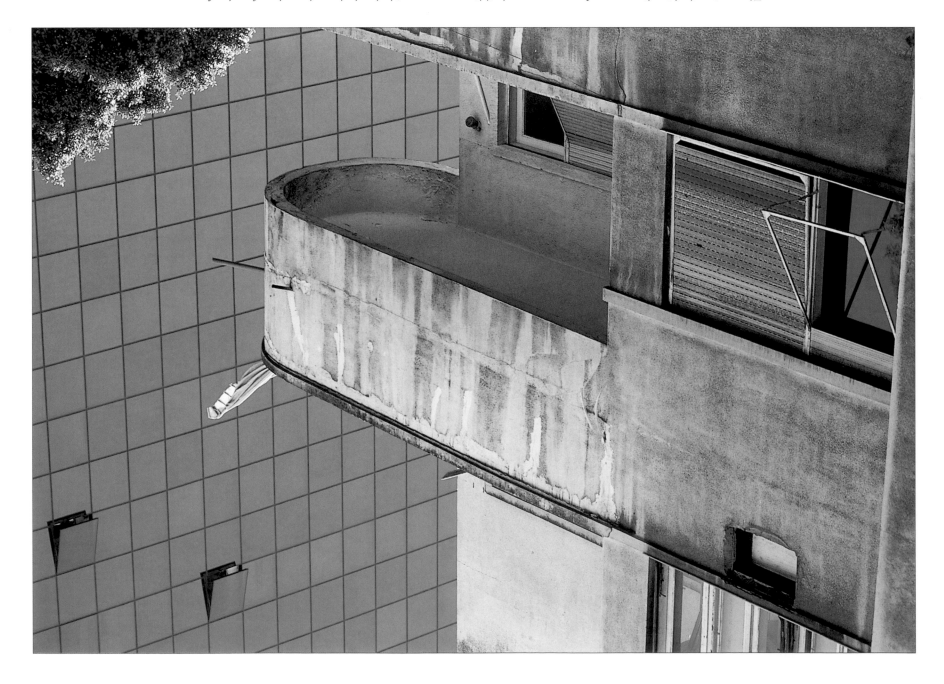

The Tel Aviv marina is at the north of the city, at the opposite end and from the port of Jaffa. One of the largest in the Middle East, the Tel Aviv marina is located alongside some of the most beautiful beaches in the Mediterranean. The city of Tel Aviv was founded along the sand dunes north of Jaffa in 1909 by a group of Jewish settlers. The name Tel Aviv means "Hill of Spring," and reflects their hope for a new future built upon the ruins of the past. Originally built as a garden suburb to the port of Jaffa, Tel Aviv has since become one of the largest Jewish cities in the world.

A fishing boat sits in dry dock in front of a row of homes in Akko. Akko is home to the Pisan Harbor, which is lined with sea walls originally built by the Crusaders. Overlooking the Mediterranean at the northern tip of Haifa Bay, Akko's architecture is a cacophony of Gothic archways, Turkish minarets, and richly eloquent views. Like Jerusalem and many other cities throughout Israel, Akko is divided into old and new cities. It also boasts a subterranean Crusader city.

ABOVE: *The Baha'i garden and shrine in Haifa, featuring the golden dome of the temple and the exquisitely manicured tropical flora and fauna that surround it. Modern Haifa has its roots in 1758 when, after many centuries of lying in ruins, this coastal town and its harbor were rebuilt by Sheik Darh Al-Omar. In the years since its rebirth Haifa has grown into a bustling port city and maritime center. It is the third-largest city in Israel and the center of the country's high-technology industry. It also is the center of the Baha'i religion, a faith based on brotherhood, love, and charity. The shrine's unusual dome and Corinthian-style columns make it the most recognized landmark in Haifa.*

RIGHT: *Places like the Mar Sabba monastery in Wadi Qilt in Samaria have been home to monks for 1,600 years. This surrealistic landscape lies where the Wadi Qilt River meets the dramatic gorge in the canyon between Jericho and Jerusalem. Here one can find tiny niches hollowed out from the rock face as isolation cells for the monks. The hills of Samaria are also home to such biblical sites as Shiloh and Jacob's Well.*

Beit Jann in Galilee is the highest village in Israel. Here elderly Druze men wearing turbans and white flowing robes continue the traditional dress that has been a part of this region for 5,000 years. This region of western Galilee is dotted with hundreds of small settlements that comprise a world unto themselves. Here mountain streams rush down the upper Galilee hills into the Jordan River, which in turn rushes southward 710 feet (222m) below sea level into the Sea of Galilee.

At Beit She'an, a newly excavated city located east of the Gilboa mountain range between the Jordan Rift, one of the lowest points in Israel, and the Beit She'an Valley, archaeologists have unearthed 6,000 years of civilization, including a nearby Roman amphitheater which once seated 8,000 people. The Jordan Rift, which stretches 4,000 miles (6,500km) from Syria to Africa, eventually crosses the lowest point on earth: the Dead Sea.

ABOVE: *This aqueduct in Caesarea was built by King Herod around 50 B.C.E. The city of Caesarea was founded by Herod and named in honor of the emperor Caesar Augustus. Around the year 6 B.C.E. it was designated the residence of the Roman governors of Judea, and for 500 years thereafter it remained the capital of Roman Palestine.*

LEFT: *A Chalcolithic dwelling, re-created from local materials, at the Golan Archaeological Museum at Katzrin, the largest commercial city in the area and the "capital" of the Golan Heights. This modern city was founded in 1977 on the site of a very ancient city of the same name. Nearby Ancient Katzrin Park is the site of an excavated Jewish village dating back to the third century B.C.E.. It is believed that at one time there were as many as twenty-seven Jewish villages of this type in the region.*

Masada, located some 1,000 feet (300m) above
the Dead Sea, is the most spectacular archeological
site in Israel. It was here on this forlorn mesa that
King Herod the Great built an impregnable fortress
to use as a retreat from his often rebellious subjects.
It was also here, in 66 C.E., that a valiant group of
Jewish rebels called the Sicarii (named after their
favored weapon, the dagger, or sica) seized control
of the fortress from the Romans and proceeded to
hold them off for several years until, when defeat
was clearly inevitable, the band of 1,000 Jews took
their own lives rather than surrender to the Romans.

Toward the end of the second century B.C.E., primarily in reaction against the Greek education that many Jews were forced to undergo, it became mandatory that Jewish boys be taught the Torah. Over the centuries this translated to an overall high esteem for education among the Jews, and by the twentieth century this has become a point of cultural pride. Today, religious studies and secular studies are a matter of course for Israeli public school students, both boys and girls.

The sight of female soldiers in the Israeli army has been commonplace for decades. Women fought alongside men in the 1948 War of Independence. Today all young men reaching the age of eighteen are automatically drafted for national service for three years, and all young women reaching the same age must serve for two. Married women are exempt from military service, as are religious women and men devoting themselves full time to religious studies or services. Non-Jews are not required to serve, but many volunteer.

A promotional photo from around 1945 depicts two girls and two women who work in the community kitchen of a Jewish settlement in Palestine. During the years between World War I and World War II, Zionist organizations dedicated to the notion of a homeland for the Jewish people capitalized on all aspects of the lives of Jewish settlers to encourage people worldwide to support their cause, both ideologically and financially.

The Star of David, a six-pointed star formed by superimposing two triangles, sometimes also called the Shield of David or Magen David, was not originally an exclusively Jewish symbol but was used by many ancient peoples. In the thirteenth century it was used as a magic symbol of the kabbalah, or Jewish mysticism. Its first official use was in the early seventeenth century, when the Jewish community of Prague adopted the Star of David as its official symbol. In the late nineteenth century it was adopted by many Zionist groups, and in 1949 it was placed upon the flag of Israel.

RIGHT: *Israel's Independence Day, or Yom HaAtzma'ut, is celebrated every year on May 14. Traditionally the day begins with hikes and picnics and ends with parties and fireworks. Here the event is being marked with an air show above the Mediterranean, as thousands of citizens watch from the beaches below.*

BELOW: *On Israeli Independence Day in 1996, students celebrated at the Western Wall, proudly waving the Israeli national flag.*

Israeli soldiers guard a border crossing to Jericho. With so many battles having been fought over the years, each one altering the shape of the State of Israel, the necessity for border guards has become a way of life. At some borders it is still advised not to get out and walk around because old, hidden land mines might be accidentally exploded.

A refugee camp is located on the outskirts of the town of Jericho, in the West Bank. Archaeological digging in the region confirms the presence of civilization here going as far back as 8,000 B.C.E. Jericho today is inhabited by roughly 7,000 people, most of whom are involved in agriculture. Safely sheltered within a green oasis surrounded on all sides by barren land, the secret to Jericho's agricultural heritage—some say it may have been the site of the the world's first agricultural community— are underground springs that feed its bounty.

A B O V E : *A home and a gorgeous tree in bloom in Jericho, in the West Bank, is yet more evidence of the abundance wrought by underground springs beneath this ancient city. Over the centuries, rulers have used Jericho as a warm-weather retreat. Indeed, Hisham, the tenth Umayyad caliph, constructed a fabulous palace about two miles (3.2km) from the city in the eighth century. The floors of the palace were covered with intricate Islamic mosaic tiles.*

R I G H T : *Jericho, which lies east of Jerusalem, is an oasis along the biblical Jericho Road, which runs through the hills of the Judean desert. This desert is home not only to Jericho, but also to the biblical towns of Bethlehem, Herodian, and Hebron.*

The Judean Desert, just east of the Judean Hills at the descent of the range into the Jordan Rift Valley, has served as a refuge for prophets, monks, and kings over the centuries. This, almost more than any other region of Israel, is the land of the Bible.

ABOVE: *The Judean hills and lowlands to the west of Jerusalem, known as Shefalah, have for centuries been the site of pine, cypress and olive groves. In recent years the region has been the target of government- and philanthropy-backed reforestation. Here it is not unusual to encounter a wide array of wildlife.*

RIGHT: *Olive groves in Samaria bear silent witness to the centuries of history that have transpired here. Samaria, both as a city and a region, figures prominently in biblical narratives about Elijah and Elisha as well as in the writings of Amos, Hosea and Isaiah. It was from here that King Herod began ruling Judea in 30 B.C.E., here where Jesus' parable of the Good Samaritan is set, and here that John the Baptist is believed to be buried.*

BELOW: *Despite adverse conditions, agriculture in Israel has advanced to a degree that compares favorably with that of most developed countries. In 1948, Israel produced only 30 percent of the food it needed, but by the 1970s was actively supplying all of its domestic fruit, vegetable, poultry, and dairy needs. Israel's chief crop is citrus fruit, but other sizable crops include cotton, peanuts, sugar beets, and sisal.*

RIGHT: *While most areas of Israel have little rainfall, some parts receive enough precipitation to support trees and wildflowers. As with plants, for people, thriving in Israel requires the abilities to adapt to sometimes harsh circumstances and to find the areas with the most hospitable climates.*

The Israeli agricultural economy is a thriving part of the nation's industry, providing more than 50 percent of the country's food needs. The legendary and unique success of cooperative farming nation-wide would not have been possible were it not for one key technological invention—drip irrigation—which made it possible for farmers to both conserve water and get it directly to the crops. Moreover, the system allows farmers to use sea water due to an inexpensive desalinization process worked out by scientists, which has meant, among other things, the blossoming of the region surrounding the salty Dead Sea.

An Israeli member of a kibbutz, or communal farm, carries ripe bananas from the field to the factory. Interestingly, many members of the nation's kibbutzim have traditionally taken leadership roles in the country's national defense. Kibbutzniks made up the lion's share of the members of the Palmach, Israel's elite fighting force in pre-state days and the predecessor to the current army. The kibbutzim have also directly influenced the country's political system, primarily in their relationship to the Labor Party.

LEFT: *A worker in a factory cuts squares of rich, nutty pastries, and prepares them for sale in the marketplace. Each of the many ethnic groups in Israel makes its own contribution to the varied cuisine of the country.*

BELOW: *A cat enjoys the smells in the spice market in Jerusalem. Spices have a long history in the region, which was the center of the spice trade between Europe and the Far East for hundreds of years.*

Shoppers in a grocery store in Jerusalem examine pieces of melon before purchasing them. Fruits and vegetables grow abundantly in Israel's moderate climate and make up a large part of the average Israeli's diet. One especially popular dish is a salad made of diced cucumbers and tomatoes, which is particularly delicious due to the excellent produce.

ABOVE: *An artist works at restoring an ancient mosaic, reconstructing a small part of Israel's rich and varied history. Great care is taken to preserve the artifacts of the many civilizations that have flourished in the land.*

RIGHT: *A painter poses by her work, an oil on canvas. Israel has a thriving artistic community, as well as a history of promoting the work of fine artists. Quite often artists have been only too glad to donate their time and their work. In 1959, for example, the Hadassah organization asked the Jewish-Russian painter Marc Chagall to design the stained glass windows for the synagogue of a new hospital, and he not only agreed to do it, but he was pleased to do it for free.*

An artist in Safed, Israel, displays his work outside his studio. Safed is 3,000 feet (900m) above sea level, Israel's most elevated city, and the seat of a great deal of Jewish mysticism. There is an artist's colony located here during the warm months, roughly July through September, when galleries display the often mystical works of the residents.

The Jordan River extends some 165 miles (265km) from the snowy peaks of Mount Hermon to the catch basin of the Dead Sea. Mark Twain wrote that the Jordan River is "so crooked that a man does not know which side of it he is on half the time. In going 90 miles it does not get over more than 50 miles of ground."

The spectacularly beautiful, rocky cliffs of the Arbel
Mount in the north of Israel near Lake Kinneret
served as a hideout for Jewish rebels in biblical
times. Today the Arbel is a popular spot for rock
climbers and hikers.

Israel features a wide variety of natural features within its small area, including the Keshet Tunnel, where rock climbers pull themselves up by ropes. Israelis tend to be enthusiastic hikers, eager to see the wonders of the country.

The canyon of Nahal Hever is home to a number of interesting sites, including the Cave of Horrors, where forty skeletons of men, women, and children dating back to the time of the Bar-Kochba revolt (135 C.E.) were discovered. The canyon is dotted with caves and, it is believed, holds many more secrets within its folds.

The rocky seaside region near Eilat, at the south-ernmost tip of Israel, formed out of Precambrian rock and shaped by the forces of nature long before the beginning of life on the planet, is a geologist's dream. Granite, gneiss, quartz-porphyry, and diabase are just a few of the rocky treasures that Eilat and the Red Sea hold.

Fed by the River Jordan, the Dead Sea is not really a sea at all: it is in fact a lake laced with minerals, many of which—potash, bromine, magnesium, and salt—are drawn in vast quantities from the Dead Sea's seemingly unlimited supply and provide Israel with a valuable resource. The area is a major tourist attraction as well as a site for cure-seekers and health enthusiasts.

The vast Negev desert constitutes some 60 percent of Israel's land area, but holds less than 10 percent of its population. The Hebrew word "negev" means "parched," and these cracked beds of earth attest to its aridness. Nevertheless, some parts of the Negev do receive as much as 12 inches (30cm) of rain every year, and still other parts support successful agricultural communities. David Ben-Gurion was such a staunch believer in the Negev that he chose to live there when he retired from politics and was buried there when he died.

ABOVE: *A mushroom-shaped rock formation in the desert is just one of the many natural beauties of this seemingly forbidding landscape. Like the native-born Israeli named for the cactus fruit, the sabra, this world is both rough and sweet.*

LEFT: *In the heart of the Negev the desert dunes and the population of Bedouin shepherds dotting the topography seem timeless. Here the eucalyptus and the tamarind tree thrive amid arid conditions. On the desk of the house where he lived in the Negev, David Ben-Gurion kept the following handwritten passage from the Old Testament: "I will even make a way in the wilderness, and rivers in the desert."*

Bibliography

Comay, Joan. *Who's Who in Jewish History*. Revised edition. Oxford University Press: 1995.

Durant, Will, and Ariel Durant. *The Story of Civilization*. 11 vols. Simon & Schuster, 1935-1975.

Harris, William H, and Judith S. Levy (eds). *The New Columbia Encyclopedia*, Columbia University Press, 1975.

Johnson, Paul. *A History of the Jews*. HarperPerennial, 1987.

Potok, Chaim. *Wanderings*. Fawcett Crest, 1978.

Roth, Cecil. *A History of the Jews*. Schocken, 1971.

—————. *The Jews in the Renaissance*. Harper & Row, 1965.

Sacher, Howard M. *A History of Israel*. Alfred A. Knopf, 1976.

Tuchman, Barbara. *Bible and Sword*. Ballantine, 1984.

Wouk, Herman. *This is My God; the Jewish Way of Life*. Revised edition Doubleday: 1984.

Further Suggested Reading

Abrahams, Israel. *Jewish Life in the Middle Ages*. Atheneum, 1969.

Albright, W.F. *The Archeology of Palestine*. Penguin, 1963.

—————. *From the Stone Age to Christianity*. 1957.

Bein, Alex, with H. Abrami. *Theodor Herzl*. Atheneum, 1970.

Ben-Gurion, David. *Rebirth and Destiny of Israel*. 1952.

—————. *Israel: Years of Challenge*. 1963.

—————. *Israel—A Personal History*. 1972.

Goldin, Judah (ed). *The Jewish Experience*. Yale University Press, 1976.

Herzl, Theodor. *Diaries*. 5 vols. Edited by Raphael Patai, translated by Harry Zohn. The Herzl Press and Thomas Yoseloff, 1960.

Kaufman, Yehezkel. *The Religion of Israel, From its Beginnings to the Babylonian Exile*. University of Chicago Press, 1960.

Maimonides. *The Guide of the Perplexed*. Translated by Shlomo Pines. University of Chicago Press, 1963.

Marcus, Jacob R. *The Jews in the Medieval World*. Harper & Row, 1965.

Roth, Cecil. *A History of the Jews in England*. Oxford University Press, 1949.

—————. *Benjamin Disraeli: Earl of Beaconsfield*. 1952.

Sanders, Ronald. *The High Walls of Jerusalem: A History of the Balfour Declaration and the Birth of the British Mandate for Palestine*. 1984.

Scholem, Gershom. *On Jews and Judaism in Crisis*. Schocken, 1976.

—————. *Major Trends in Jewish Mysticism*. Schocken, 1971.

—————. *Sabbatai Sevi*. Princeton University Press, 1973.

Starr, Chester G. *A History of the Ancient World*. Oxford University Press, 1965.

Trilling, Lionel. *Mind in the Modern World*, Harcourt Brace Jovanovich, 1973.

Weizmann, Chaim. *Trial and Error*, 1949.

Index

Photography Credits

© Bill Aron: pp. 1, 58, 60, 61, 64, 65, 95

Art Resource: ©Erich Lessing: pp. 6-7, 13, 14, 16; Jewish Museum: p. 12, 19, 28, 29, 30; Snark: p. 27

AP/Wide World Photos: pp. 51, 53, 68, 70, 72, 74, 94

Corbis Bettmann: pp. 10, 20, 22, 23, 35, 36, 38, 39, 45

© Robert Fried: pp. 73 right, 83, 89, 99, 100

FPG International Corp.: pp. 31, 37, 42; © Louis Goldman: pp. 63, 73 left; © Bob Higbee: p. 2-3, 104

© Beryl Goldberg: pp. 5 top, 76, 77, 88-89, 98, 113

Itamar Grinberg: pp. 5 bottom, 66, 69, 78 top, 79, 81, 82, 85, 86, 87, 90-91, 93, 97, 106, 110 left, 112 top, 114, 115, 116-117, 120-121, 124-125, 125

Israel Ministry of Tourism: p. 109

Leo de Wys Inc.: © Van Phillips: p. 21

© Richard T. Nowitz: pp. 54-55, 71, 96, 101, 102-103, 105, 107, 123

© Zev Radovan: pp. 9, 11, 15, 18, 24, 25, 26, 33, 44, 84, 118-119, 122

Reuters/Corbis-Bettmann: p. 50

Courtesy of United Jewish Appeal: pp. 40, 43, 46; © Yosefa Drescher: p. 75; © Joel Fishman: p. 52; © Joseph Neumayer: p. 41; © Zion M. Ozeri: pp. 62-63, 78 bottom, 92, 108, 112 bottom

UPI/ Corbis-Bettmann: pp. 17, 32, 34, 47, 48, 49

© David H. Wells: pp. 8, 56-57, 57, 58-59, 67, 80, 110 right, 111